NATIONALISM AND EDUCATION IN MODERN CHINA

Nationalism and Education in Modern China

BY

CYRUS H. PEAKE

NEW YORK

Howard Fertig

1970

TO
MY PARENTS

PREFACE

In the writing of this book I have tried to divest myself of national prejudice and recount objectively the development of the spirit of nationalism and militarism in China as it has been reflected in the evolving modern educational system. Most of the research was done in China while on leave of absence from Columbia University as Cutting Travelling Fellow during the year 1928-1929. No attempt has been made to recount developments since that time.

It is with a deep feeling of gratitude that I acknowledge my indebtedness to Professor Carlton J. H. Hayes of Columbia University, whose lectures and published works on modern nationalism led me to undertake this study; to Professor J. J. L. Duyvendak of the University of Leyden and Visiting Professor of Chinese at Columbia, whose innumerable criticisms and suggestions have added immeasurably to the value and accuracy of this study; to Mr. L. C. Goodrich of the Department of Chinese and to Dr. Arthur W. Hummel, Chief of the Division of Chinese Literature of the Congressional Library and Visiting Lecturer in Chinese at Columbia for the years 1930-1932, who have read the manuscript and given it their valued criticisms; to Mr. T. L. Yuan, Associate Director of the National Library of Peiping, who so kindly placed at my disposal the rich resources of that Library; to Mr. W. Y. Yen, Cataloger of the National Library of Peiping, who as Curator of the Chinese collection at Columbia during the years 1930-1932 gave generously of his time, especially in the preparation of the list of Chinese characters in Appendix II; to T. A. Bisson, Dr. Shepard B. Clough, C. C. Wang, and Wilbur L. Williams for the care with which they have read the page proof, and to my wife whose constant interest has been a source of inspiration and who has assisted extensively in the preparation of the manuscript for publication.

CYRUS H. PEAKE

COLUMBIA UNIVERSITY
    January, 1932

CONTENTS

INTRODUCTION

Perhaps in no other phase of the modern transformation which China is undergoing has there been such consistent and, on the whole, progressive development as in the field of education. A survey, therefore, of the successive aims, curricula and, finally, of the textbooks used in the schools will be not only a clue to the mental attitudes of the coming generation of Chinese, but will also afford a reflection of the dominant philosophies and objectives of the politicians and educators of the past and present generations. The period covered by this study extends from 1860 to 1930. Matters of interest to educators from a professional point of view, such as finance, administration, and pedagogics will be only indirectly touched upon. It is the thesis of this study that the dominant motive and aim of those Chinese, who have been responsible for the introduction of modern education into China in the course of the past seventy years, was to build a strong nation resting on military power and capable of existing in a world of warring nations. A system of modern education was conceived of at the beginning by the official ruling class as a most effective means of strengthening the nation. Later, accompanying the rise of the spirit of modern nationalism, a national educational system was asserted to be the exclusive prerogative of the state, to serve as a tool in its unification and an aid in gaining for it a place of equality among the nations. All other aims that normally accompany the conception of universal, democratic and compulsory education such as the removal of illiteracy, the strengthening of the economic power of the individual and of society were subservient and secondary.

The control of this evolving modern educational system by politicians and bureaucrats caused it to be under the constant influence of changing political fortunes of the nation, which resulted in frequent changes of personnel among the higher and more influential educational officials. This in turn resulted in as many changes in administrative forms, curricula, aims, and textbooks. However, through all this outer change the one dominant motive remained. With the rise of the spirit and philosophy of modern nationalism the desire on the part of China's new leaders to develop a state-controlled educational system, subservient to the nationalistic ideal, achieved an almost religious intensity. After 1925 the educational system became permeated with the dogmatic and intolerant spirit of modern nationalism. The steps by which this came about will be especially emphasized in what is to follow. That modern nationalism in China, as is usually the case elsewhere, is an intolerant cult may be seen in the fierce and successful attack upon schools conducted by Christians, Mohammedans and Buddhists, as well as upon the old-fashioned Confucian type of school. In all this China has placed itself in line with many western nations where a government-controlled system of education is permeated with a similar nationalistic spirit.

Indeed, Chinese politicians and bureaucrats, and those educators who had perforce to follow their lead, though often reluctantly, consciously imitated the Japanese, and in the West the Germans and the French, in this respect, and set about artificially to propagate, through the educational system, a nationalistic spirit.

The study is divided into five chapters and two appendices. The first chapter covers the period from 1860 to 1894 and outlines the beginnings of modern education. The second chapter does the same for the period from 1895 to 1911, when the first modern system of education was adopted and a modern Ministry of Education established on a basis of equality with the other government ministries. The third chapter continues the survey of educational aims and curricula from the establishment of the Republic to the present. The fourth chapter is devoted to a survey of the methods employed by the Ministry of Education to control the publication of textbooks. The final chapter, in a summary way, traces the rise of modern nationalism and its influence on the educational system. The first appendix gives a digest of the textbooks used in the Mass Education Movement and in the primary and middle schools from 1905 to 1929. The second appendix is made up of the Chinese characters used in this book, arranged alphabetically under the Romanized form.

At the outset the author wishes to make clear that in dealing thus critically with such a sensitive and live issue as Chinese nationalism, he is not doing so as an American nationalist, but rather as a student of the world-wide phenomenon of modern nationalism. That the intolerant attitudes toward other nations and peoples inculcated by the school systems of most nations is a serious bar to international coöperation is now a widely recognized fact. In this connection it is significant to note that Baron Shidehara, Foreign Minister of Japan, in his official statement of policy regarding the Manchurian crisis in the fall of 1931 stated, "Unfortunately . . . feelings antagonistic to Japan have been openly encouraged in school textbooks and have become deeply seated in the Chinese mind."

It is easy to understand why and how the Chinese have imitated the West in this respect, but to understand in such a case does not mean to condone. Indeed, it seems but the more tragic that this should have come about when one reflects upon the richness of certain universal conceptions set forth by Chinese philosophers through the centuries. The author cherishes the belief that the present period, marked by the expression of an intolerant form of nationalism, may pass and that the Chinese will yet contribute constructively to the realization of the World Community.

Chapter I

MODERN EDUCATION IN CHINA AND ITS AIMS
1860-1895

In the course of the forty-five years, between the close of the second disastrous struggle with the western nations and the establishment of the modern system of education accompanied by the abolition of the century-old system of civil service examinations, the Chinese and Manchu officials had but one dominant aim which was to modernize and strengthen their military and naval forces in order to preserve the Empire. Only as much of western educational material and technique was to be introduced as would help to realize that aim. The old traditions and classical literature and culture were to remain intact, together with the traditional conception of education as being simply a preparation for entering official life through the door of the civil service examinations. From out of the mass of the Chinese population men of talent were to be selected for the service of the Empire.

The contrast between this aim and the dominant aims of modern educational systems is here apparent. In fact a universal system of compulsory education, such as has developed among the leading nations of the West in modern times, never existed in China. The only approach to such a system, in recent centuries, lay in the officially supported *Shu Yüan* or Provincial Colleges together with the *Kuo Tzŭ Chien* or

National College and the Hanlin Academy located at the capital. In these institutions a few select and advanced scholars assembled for further study and examination under government patronage. Education of the youth was left almost entirely to the village, the clan and the family under a system of private tutors or teachers directly engaged by the elders. The competitive civil service examinations required of successful candidates a thorough knowledge of the Classics. As a consequence the curriculum in the private schools, where the study and memorizing of the classical books consumed the greater part of the students' time, was determined by the examination system. The students who failed to pass the examinations or did not secure official positions, and they constituted by far the greater majority, found a livelihood in commercial pursuits or in serving as scribes or secretaries in the provincial and local government bureaus. Only a rough estimate of the percentage of literacy can be made in the absence of comprehensive and accurate statistics, but certainly it did not exceed 10 per cent of the population and probably was somewhat less. Numbers, however, are no guide in estimating the great influence of the civil service examination system, together with the numerous private schools, in holding the Chinese people together under the Empire through the centuries. In view of that fact, it is not surprising that the officials were slow to abolish the examination system, striving for a time to effect a compromise.

This compromise was well summarized by an epigram widely repeated during the years prior to the 1911 Revolution. It was commonly attributed to Chang Chih-tung, one of the most progressive and enlightened Chinese statesmen of the nineteenth century: "Chung hsüeh wei chu; hsi hsüeh wei yung."[1] The thought implied was that though western science was to be adopted for practical purposes, Chinese learning should remain the guide.

This narrow, pragmatic view of the value of western education meant that at first only as much of it would be officially allowed as aimed directly at modernizing the army and the navy and strengthening the defenses of the Empire. The bitter experience of two defeats at the hands of the westerners had borne in on the minds of the more conservative officials, at least on a few who were able to make their will effective, the necessity of change and of going to school to the West. Arsenals were established in a number of important centers in the Empire, such as at Foochow and Shanghai, for the purpose of turning out modern armaments and munitions.[2]

The spirit in which western science was introduced into governmental institutions at this time reveals the same narrow aim. "In 1865," writes Dr. W. A. P. Martin, "it was resolved by the Tsungli Yamen to raise the school of interpreters *(T'ung Wên Kuan)* to the rank of a college by adding a scientific department and admitting students of high attainments in Chinese learning."[3] Prince Kung, President of the Tsungli Yamen (bureau controlling foreign affairs), presented, in 1865, the memorial which resulted in the enlargement of the College. "We believe that in order to manufacture machines, lectures and research in mathematics and astronomy must be provided for." Li Hung-chang and Tso Tsung-t'ang realized this when providing for such instruction in their arsenals (at Shanghai and Foochow respectively). "Tso selects young men of good families and appoints foreigners to teach them languages, mathematics and drawing as a fundamental prerequisite for the construction of steamships." Of course it is possible to rent ships and buy arms, but then we would never be able to construct our own and ". . . the secrets (of such construction) will remain with others. . . ."

In order to make the adoption of western science more acceptable to the haughty conservatives, Prince Kung artfully relied upon historical argument.

We find [upon searching into antiquity] that Western sciences borrowed their roots from ancient Chinese mathematics. Westerners still regard their mathematics as coming from the Orient. It is only because of the careful, inquiring nature of the Westerners that they are good at developing something new out of the old. . . . China invented the method, Westerners adopted it. . . . Moreover, the Emperor K'ang Hsi [1662-1723] was deeply versed in Western science. During his reign mathematical studies were connected with the Astronomical Board. . . . In former times the farmers and soldiers all knew astronomy, but in later times it was prohibited and only a few knew it [those connected with the Court]. During K'ang Hsi's time the prohibition against private astronomical observations was removed with the result that a greater and more widespread interest in it developed. Scholars who studied the Classics knew something about mathematics as well and there were many works published which dealt with it in detail. It was commonly said, "If there is only one thing a scholar does not know, therein lies his shame."

It is wrong, therefore, to say that it is a shame to follow westerners and study their science. Western countries learn from each other and daily their science develops, while Japan learns from them all. Recently Japan has appointed men to study in England. For all of these reasons the *T'ung Wên Kuan* should become a college, teaching western sciences and especially mathematics and astronomy, while members of the

Hanlin Academy, comprising the foremost scholars in the land, should be permitted to study at the institution.[4]

Initial support for the plan to introduce the teaching of pure science into China came from provinical officials. The provincial governors, Li Hung-chang and Tso Tsung-t'ang, as we have already seen, realized the value and necessity of teaching science at their arsenals in Shanghai and Foochow respectively. Intimate contact with foreigners had converted them to it. Closely associated with them was one of the greatest officials of the time Tsêng Kuo-fan, who had just completed the suppression of the great T'ai-p'ing rebellion. Toward the close of the rebellion foreign-trained troops had played a helping part and no doubt Tsêng was impressed by the effectiveness of their modern weapons.[5] Convinced of their superiority, this conservative old official became an active supporter of the introduction of western science as it immediately related to the arts of war. This is seen in the fact that at this time (1865) he caused to be published from his headquarters at Nanking a translation of the fifteen chapters of Euclid's *Elements of Geometry.*[6]

The circumstances resulting in the translation into Chinese of Euclid's Geometry are most interesting as a reflection of the spirit of the times. These are recounted in the five prefaces appearing in the edition which Tsêng Kuo-fan ordered printed in 1865. The prefaces were written by Tsêng,[7] Matteo Ricci, Hsü Kwang-ch'i, Alexander Wylie, and Li Shan-lan. Tsêng informs us that,

The first six chapters of the *Chi Ho Yüan Pên* (Euclid's Geometry) were taught to Hsü Kwang-ch'i [a prominent official at the close of the Ming dynasty and a member of a wealthy and influencial family] by the foreigner Matteo Ricci. During the

Hsien Fêng period [1851-1862] Li Shan-lan of Haining began, with the Western scholar Alexander Wylie, the translation of the last nine chapters and the correction of the first six chapters. Thus was the work [begun 250 years earlier] completed. Han Lu-ch'ing of Sungkiang published it, but shortly thereafter the wood blocks were burned in the course of the (T'ai-p'ing) rebellion. Li Shan-lan, who worked under me in the Anking army, showed me the work saying, "This work is indispensable to mathematicians. It will be lost if it is not printed at once."[8] I moved my headquarters [Tsêng was then bringing his successful campaigns against the rebels to a close] to Chinling [Nanking] and ordered Li to correct the last nine chapters and to have them printed . . . and to do the same for the first six chapters as well.

Tsêng then proceeds to survey the development of Chinese mathematics and to point out its inherent defect.

According to our traditional mathematics each section derives its name from a specific [practical] function.[9] The students all follow rules in solving their problems. All their lives they use mathematics knowing only how to do it and not why it is done. Therefore, they consider mathematics as a very difficult subject simply because they are confused, knowing the method, but not the principle. . . . Euclid's Geometry [on the other hand] deals not with method, but with principles. . . .

Therefore, he concludes that it should be studied first and for that reason it should be printed.

Another factor that won Viceroy Tsêng's support of the project no doubt arose out of the argument set forth by Matteo Ricci in his own preface to his translation of the first six chapters. After pointing out that the difference between arithmetic and geometry was that the former dealt with practical problems and the latter with fundamental principles, Ricci dilated on the practical advantages of a knowledge of geometry. He pointed out its value to astronomy, to the making of the calendar, to medicine, to geography, to commerce, etc.[10] Above all, he argued, it was most essential in the conduct of military affairs.[11] "Military affairs are the most important of all in the nation for upon them its security depends. . . . Therefore, a general of wisdom and bravery must first of all have a knowledge of geometry, otherwise his knowledge and bravery will be without practical value. . . ." In the West ". . . before Christianity became widespread . . ." one nation fought another, but often the smaller one conquered the larger because its military leader possessed a knowledge of geometry.

The publication of this work by so renowned an official as Tsêng Kuo-fan played an important rôle in paving the way for the first significant change in the civil-service examinations since the introduction of the *Pa Ku Wên Chang* in the Ming dynasty.[12] This change, by which science became an optional subject in an examination which the candidate voluntarily chose, occured in 1887. Dr. Martin, the President of the Imperial college (*T'ung Wên Kuan*) in summing up its work wrote, "Its principal achievement . . . is the introduction (though limited) of science into the civil-service examination. This measure, decreed in 1887, had been under deliberation for twenty years; governors and viceroys had recommended it, but it was not adopted until the government obtained, through our college, some conception of the nature and scope of modern science."[13] It is significant that the first memorial advocating the change was presented by Tso Tsung-t'ang, who was in charge of the arsenal at Foochow. Viceroy Li Hung-chang memorialized the Throne in 1875 advocating the same change and adding physical sciences to the mathematical subjects which Tso had previously suggested. The first triennial examination following this change came in 1888. The Jesuit Father, Etienne Zi, describes the nature and origin of this change as follows:[14]

The thirteenth year of Kuang Hsü (1887) at the suggestion of the Imperial Censor Chên Hsiu-ying, it was decided that in the examination *Ching Ku Ch'ang* [an examination for Bachelors on the Classics and Antiquity], the provincial examiners should offer some questions in mathematics to the Bachelors who wished to answer them. Copies of those papers answered correctly were sent to the Tsungli Yamen, which called the authors, prior to the examination for the Doctorate [held in Peking], to a second examination in mathematics. Those who passed this examination successfully were presented by the Yamen to the Shun T'ien Fu [Prefecture of Peking] for the doctoral examination.

Tsêng Kuo-fan directly supported the establishment of both the Foochow and Shanghai arsenals. In 1867 he ordered General Tso Tsung-t'ang, who had been closely associated with him in the suppression of the T'ai-p'ing rebellion, to coöperate with the Frenchman M. Prosper Giquel in founding the College for Marine Navigation and Engineering at Foochow. Yung Wing, China's first returned student in modern times, working under Tsêng's orders established, in coöperation with the Tao-t'ai (ranking officer) of Shanghai, a similar school and arsenal in that port. John Fryer was for thirty years in charge of the translation bureau connected with the arsenal. In the course of that time ". . . an encyclopedia of some hundreds of volumes of standard treatises (was published) which found its way all over China and even to Japan."[15] According to a catalogue published in 1905, in the period from 1870 to 1904, 178 works were published including a quarterly on Current Affairs in the West.[10] A majority of these works were translations: 88 English, 19 American, 3 French, 5 Japanese, and 2 German. Fryer, himself, was responsible for translating most of those from English and American sources. The range of subjects covered was considerable including works on law, government, surgery, agriculture, chemistry, mathematics, railroading, naval affairs, ship construction, etc., astronomy, telegraphy, the construction of gas engines and maps. The volumes were very well illustrated and beautifully printed. Associated with him in the translation bureau at one time or another were the two eminent scholar-missionaries Alexander Wylie and John Macgowan.[17]

Each year from 1872 to 1875 a group of 30 students was sent to America by the Government under the guardianship of Yung Wing. The students remained in America but a few years when a reaction among officials at Peking, born of a fear that they were becoming indoctrinated with revolutionary Republican ideas, caused their recall (1881) before they had finished their courses. They returned to find the way blocked for their employment and advancement in government service and it was only after 1900 that any of them commenced to emerge as leaders. John Fryer, writing in 1897, stated that ". . . only a few of them have made any good use of the elementary education received. Similar commissions on a smaller scale were sent to England, France and Germany, with about equally unsatisfactory results."[18] Fryer's statement as to the accomplishments of the returned students at the time was true enough, but since 1900 when the spirit of reform was in the air more of them came to the fore as leaders.

In 1874 a Polytechnic Institution, with a reading-room, was established in Shanghai from funds subscribed chiefly by high officials. For many years it published themes on modern subjects written by the students. By 1897 there were eight Chinese and eight foreign members on its Committee.[19]

At Tientsin in the year 1885 there was established the first modern military school in China. It was the work of Li Hung-chang, then Viceroy of Chihli Province. The project received Imperial sanction following his memorial advocating it.

Last year [August 1884] I received an Imperial decree ordering me to select and employ German military officers at Tientsin. As soon as they arrived they were diligently to train officers (for the new army). I have already, in a subsequent memorial, reported that this has been done. These (German) officers are expert not only in gun-drill and in the movement of troops, but also skilled in the method of erecting gun-placements and in making camps. They are all graduates of German military academies. . . . [A number of the foremost military commanders of China] . . . have recommended to me the establishment of a system of military schools modelled after those in the West employing in them German officers as instructors. The students for these schools should be selected from among the more intelligent and physically sound soldiers in the camps. This I agreed should be done. I thereupon ordered [a number of these provincial commanders] to select a group of non-commissioned officers and privates to be sent to the school (at Tientsin) to be trained (as officers). I discover that military developments in western countries are constantly improving. Their admirals and naval officers must come from Naval Academies and their generals and military officers must come from Military Academies. Therefore, they are always efficient in fighting as their birth and training make them so. I hear that their military schools are very numerous and their organization is on a vast scale. There is a special place [in each school] for reading and for drawing; for studying and for practising the various military arts. Only the young and intelligent sons of the best families are selected as students and trained while they are young. When they are grown (and their training completed) they are sent to a squad in the brigade. Then, upon the recommendation of their sergeant they may [later] be made officers. . . . During the early part of their training the students live side by side in the dormitories. They are instructed in special classes in the proper way of arranging forces for battle, in the strategy of the attack and of the defense. They come to regard these matters as vital as life itself and they constantly study with all their energy. They become especially good in the proper handling of the gun and in the quick manoeuvres of the drill. If we do not know all the strong points of the enemy we cannot conquer him. Therefore, at the present time, when we are talking about military preparedness, then we should in turn learn the enemy's methods in order to control him. . . .

I discussed the plan (to have soldiers come from the camps to be trained at Tientsin) with the Commissioner of Customs of Tientsin, Tao-t'ai Chou Fu and others. We decided to place the students temporarily in the Tientsin Naval Headquarters. We decided to call the school the Military Preparatory School (*Wu Pei Hsüeh T'ang*) and to appoint the German military officers as instructors. Also we decided to appoint those proficient in foreign languages to be translators. Beginning with the first month of this year (1885) Tao-t'ai Chou Fu carefully examined the non-commissioned officers and soldiers sent from the various camps, selecting one hundred of the stronger and more intelligent ones to study at the school. *Among those chosen were some civil officers who wished to acquire military training.* (Italics mine.) Also I ordered the Tao-t'ai to draw up, in collaboration with the German officers, rules and regulations that the students might be strictly trained. For several months (after entering) the students should be required to attend classes regularly.

After a year of vigorous training in all the arts of war according to the ". . . latest Western methods . . ." the students were to be sent back to their camps and a new group sent up to form the second class. After a time when more money might be available ". . . a special academy *(Shu Yüan)* should be established and the students should be selected from the younger members of high-standing families. After being trained they should be sent to the camps to be placed in charge of companies in order to have actual experience. In this way military leadership will daily increase without limit." Students, while at the school, were to receive free tuition, board, and room. All expenses of the school—except the salaries of the German officers and the translators, who were to be paid by the central government—were to come from the North China Coastal Defense funds. In conclusion Li asserts,

This type of school provides the best means of training military officers. It is the first time one has been established in China. Therefore, being a new development it is not well-known. In order to increase the interest in it special inducements must be offered. Instructors, translators, and well-qualified students should be recommended, as has been the practise in the *T'ung Wên Kuan,* every two years to the Throne, thereby encouraging them to expend their best efforts. Those on duty will work hard and strive to succeed and thus will quicker results be attained.[20]

This petition, which met with support from the Throne, was indeed a significant one. It marked the beginning of the militarization of China along modern lines. The military forces, especially the Manchu Bannermen, had degenerated to a very low point indeed, as the exigencies of the T'aip'ing rebellion and the struggles with the foreigners had revealed.[21] The idea, then, of broadly training students in literature and science took hold easily enough under the constant threat of absorption by the western powers. The progressive militarization of the nation along western lines will be outlined below. It has been a gradual and steady process to the present. We now find the new Nationalist government of China requiring military drill of all students in the middle schools and colleges of the nation.

One or two other official schools established in this period were a further indication of the technical, practical nature of the modern educational aims held by the government prior to the war with Japan. At Wuchang the progressive Viceroy, Chang Chih-tung, had established a railroad engineering college, a mining college with some thirty students under an English professor, and schools for the study of English, French, German and Russian languages as well as general science.[22] In 1879 a telegraph school was opened in Tientsin. This school was a marked success, with some fifty students in attendance. In 1877 thirty Chinese engineers went to England, Germany and France to study, and returned in 1880. In 1881 an admiral, sixteen officers and two hundred marines went to London to study naval tactics.[23] About 1890 a naval college was founded at Nanking. The British Naval Service furnished it with two professors.[24]

This completes the list of the more important officially established institutions of modern education up to the time of the war with Japan.[25] Most of the institutions, as can readily be seen, were of a technical and military nature. Modern education was officially sought before 1894 as a means of warding off foreign encroachments. However, it was so conservative, even in this restricted technical and military sphere that, after thirty years of sporadic effort to modernize the defense forces of the Empire, the Chinese suffered a quick defeat at the hands of their more efficient and energetic neighbors, the Japanese.

If the conservative government had gone so far as to establish a few modern schools one may safely judge that modern educational ideas were spreading through the country affecting the thinking of thousands of intellectuals. Indeed the sudden development of modern education after 1895, and especially after 1900, can only be accounted for in this way.[26] Books commenced to appear in the Chinese language, apart from those published at the government arsenals and by the *T'ung Wên Kuan,* giving general accounts of Western lands, describing their educational as well as their governmental and industrial systems. General and inaccurate as they were they stirred the imagination and suggested ways by which the nation might escape from the perils that beset it.

As early as 1873 one such book appeared describing European school systems, especially that of Germany. This book, *Western Schools and Principles of Education,* was written in Chinese by the well-known German missionary Dr. Ernst Faber (Hua Chih An).[27] The preface to this work was written by Li Shan-lan, who at the time was professor of mathematics at the *T'ung Wên Kuan.* Therein he asserted that Germany's recent victories (over Austria and France) were owing to the fact that its soldiers were educated and had ideals and principles for which to fight. He stated further that there were schools everywhere in Germany and that there was no phase of human activity or interest which did not have its special school or department. Furthermore, students specially trained in these various schools pursued in later life, professions for which they had studied. Then, too, ". . . all children over eight years of age must go to school . . ." and if they do not ". . . their parents will be punished."

During the years 1880-1882 Dr. W.A.P. Martin, President of the *T'ung Wên Kuan,* traveled under orders from the

Imperial Government, through seven countries for the purpose of reporting upon their educational systems. This report was published in Peking in 1883.[28] From the pens of Chinese, official and non-official, resident or traveling abroad, came books, articles, memorials, etc., advancing plans for educational reform based upon their own personal observations. Still another very important source of influence stemmed from the modern schools that had been established by the missionaries in China. Missionary-educators, as we shall have occasion to point out below, became intimately associated with the Chinese officials in establishing the beginnings of a modern educational system. The influence of missionaries like Young J. Allen and Dr. Timothy Richard, as well as of Doctors Martin and Faber, Wylie and others, upon the early Chinese reform movement was profound indeed. In an interview which the editor of the Hongkong newspaper *China Mail* had with K'ang Yu-wei, the former asked the great reformer whence came his information and his inspiration. K'ang replied, "I owe my conversion to reform chiefly to the writings of two missionaries, the Reverend Timothy Richard and the Reverend Dr. Young J. Allen."[29]

Further evidence of the rapidly developing desire for educational reform may be found in the following comment of a missionary, who writing in 1893 stated, "We sometimes have men call upon us who are very well versed in science and mathematics, who have obtained their knowledge through the medium of books alone. Among the official classes, also, there is a great awakening and an increasing interest in our schools."[30] John C. Ferguson writing in 1892 pointed out that great unrest existed in Chinese literary circles, that there was an "... immense sale of all kinds of mathematical and scientific books; that the majority of students in the modern technical schools are sons of literary men; and above all that . . . criticism is rife as to the outrageous and severe requirements of the standard *Wên Chang*. . . . There are many and frequent complaints at the present time both among the official and literary classes, but all seem unable to do anything."[31] Another scholar-missionary, A. P. Parker, after describing the government colleges in Soochow stated that in 1893 subjects concerning current affairs were ". . . frequently given out in the examinations . . ." as for example: The Best Methods of Military Defense; the Conservation of Waterways; China's Relations with Foreign Countries, etc.[32]

Until 1894 the beginnings of modern education were to be found in the larger metropolitan centers and the cities along the coast such as Tientsin, Shanghai, Canton and Foochow. In the *Shên-pao*, a Chinese daily in Shanghai, there appeared a long article on education, in August 1893, which pointed out the necessity for spreading a knowledge of western affairs. The article mentioned some of the schools established by the Chinese such as the *Kuang Fang Yen Kuan*, or language school, at Shanghai.[33] This school was founded for the purpose of instructing students in current affairs. The government saw the value of modern trained men and even selected a few graduates of the school for positions in the army and navy. But only a few were so selected. The rest were cut off from promotion and positions in the government with the result that they lost interest. To remedy the situation the general manager of the Shanghai school, Tao-t'ai Liu K'ang-hou suggested in a memorial that the students be permitted to take the civil service examinations, or teach, or be sent abroad as interpreters. The article stated ". . . the Civil

Service Examination ought to take pattern from those of Western lands, where nothing but what is solid and real counts for anything." It derided the *"Wên Changs"* as leading to ". . . mere empty words and no acts." In western lands each was examined according to his specialty.[34]

Another Chinese writer about the same time wrote in the *Hu-pao*, a Shanghai newspaper, that the results obtained from new schools established by the government at Tientsin, Foochow and Nanking to train men to meet the demands of the new day were unsatisfactory. "Only about three-tenths of them have been of any use to the country." The reason the others fail was held to be due to the fact that they must first study English in order to get science. So as a remedy the writer suggested that the government employ more foreigners like Edkins, Fryer and Martin to translate books; and also to have science and foreign affairs made an integral part of the curricula of the provincial colleges *(Shu Yüan)*.[35]

By way of summary: the status of modern education in China at the outbreak of the war with Japan was by no means firm or efficient. The policy of the government to adopt modern education only to the extent necessary to provide an army and navy—with the exceptions of a telegraph school at Tientsin, and a mining and commercial school at Wuhan— was narrow and conservative. The war clearly revealed the lack of development after thirty years of effort in these restricted realms. Meanwhile, in extra-official circles, books were being read dealing with modern science, mathematics, history, military science and education in Japan and the West. Many of these books had been translated into Chinese by missionaries, while some were written by Chinese who had been abroad. A few progressive and patriotic Chinese were formulating new programs and safely presenting them through the newly rising modern press, to the public and the official world from the shelter of the foreign concessions. The effects of their labors were to be noted in the years following the humiliating defeat at the hands of the Japanese in the war of 1894-1895.

CHAPTER II

MODERN EDUCATION IN CHINA AND ITS AIMS
1895-1911

The war with Japan lasted less than a year, and from the outset it was apparent that the traditional inefficiency of the Chinese mandarinate was a poor match for the highly efficient Japanese. The defeat had a deep and far-reaching effect in more accurately informed Chinese circles. In the political realm it accelerated the reform movement, which up to 1894 was confined to small groups chiefly under the leadership of Sun Yat-sen and others associated with him at that time whose activities were largely restricted to the port cities of China and to Japan.[1] The newly arising Chinese press was predominately in favour of reform carrying critical articles which were frequently anti-Manchu. The newspapers and periodicals printed in the protected port areas under foreign control adopted a fearless reform policy.[2] In the educational sphere progressive officials, whose number now rapidly increased, and reformers as well, saw the necessity for a thorough-going change in the traditional curriculum, and in the examination system. The modern educational system of Japan was to be the model for reform. The cannons of war had scarcely cooled when many memorials were presented to the Throne respectfully pointing out the need for educational reform. Many who had secretly desired such change before the war now boldly came forth.

The number of these memorials was large. The *Kwang Hsü Tung Hua Hsü Lu,* an official collection of Chinese governmental documents, gives about twenty-five of the more important ones for the period 1895 to 1898, including the Hundred Days' Reform, when the Emperor Kwang Hsü, in the summer of 1898, made an earnest, though short-lived, attempt to modernize the Empire.[3] In general these memorials aimed to introduce western science, geography, mathematics, and modern languages into the curricula, but favoured retaining the classics as the basis of education. The intention was, as formerly, to cultivate men of talent. No desire appeared in official circles during this period for compulsory universal education. The decrees issued as a result of these memorials favoured, above all, military education thus continuing with greater vigor the pre-war educational policy. However, imperial sanction was given to the establishment of a number of modern colleges, and permission was granted to introduce modern subjects into the old *Shu Yüan* or provincial colleges.[4] This step was a direct outcome of the war and a frank recognition that something more than a modernized army and navy was needed to save the Empire. An examination in more detail of a few outstanding memorials and the decrees sanctioning the suggestions therein presented will reveal the temper and spirit of the time as it affected official circles.

Japan's military success led to increased activities in the direction of developing a modern army and navy. Ministerial Vice-President Hsü Ching-têng, in 1894 pointed out in a memorial that in Germany nobles and common people alike entered military camps, and suggested that the restrictions on entrance to the Eight Banners[5] or the Manchu force, be lessened in accordance with this principle. He submitted a plan for the improvement and modernization of this deteriorating force.[6] In 1896, and again in 1899, Chang Chih-tung petitioned for the establishment of military schools after the model of those of Germany requesting that German military officers be invited to come and instruct the students. His earlier memorial which received Imperial sanction March 23, 1896 ran as follows:

I have trained a modern army [for] National Defense employing German generals and officers. . . . [The reason why Germany's army is foremost among those of the Western nations] . . . is not only because everyone in the nation is a soldier, but also because there is sufficient leadership due to the practise of training all commissioned and non-commissioned officers in military schools. Now if we wish to adopt the German military system and develop a strong army, then more [military] schools must be established and strict training enforced or capable generals will not be forthcoming. In 1885 there was established at Tientsin a Military Preparatory Academy. At that time I was Viceroy of the Liang Kwang provinces where I also established an army school. The officers of [the present] modern army were trained in these two schools, though their number is limited. . . . Now it is urgent that we should expand this method (of training officers, who in turn train the troops). . . .

Chang then proceeded to present his plan to convert a former naval school at Nanking into a military school, sending to Germany for five German officers as instructors. One hundred and fifty young men between the ages of thirteen and twenty were to be selected as students. All important departments of military training were to be provided for at the school. "Following the regulations of the *T'ung Wên Kuan,* after the students have remained for three years at the school they should be given certificates and prizes and then assigned to duties commensurate with their abilities at the camps. Thus an example would be set to stimulate those at the school to greater effort and encourage others to come to the school." This method of encouragement, which in reality placed the military officials on the same plane with the civil, he asserted to be ". . . a most vital point in the achievement of a state of military preparedness." The memorial concluded with a plan for the conducting of a railroad school in connection with the military school and for securing funds to run both. In his second memorial he stated that it was easier to establish schools then as more students were seeking admission, as they were assured of a lucrative career to which increasing social approbation was being given. Contact with the West and more especially the war with Japan, together with the scheme, first put into practise by Li Hung-chang at his military academy in Tientsin in 1886, of according to military officers the same rewards, honors and opportunities as were formerly reserved for civil authorities only, had by this time commenced to bear fruit.[7]

The war with Japan greatly stimulated the efforts of Chinese officials to develop a modern navy as well as a modern army. The Tsungli Yamen memorialized the Throne, in the summer of 1896, to the effect that on June 2, 1896 it had received from the Council of State a copy of a memorial submitted by Pien Pao-ch'üan, Viceroy of Fukien and Chekiang provinces, in which he reported the results of his investigation of conditions at the Foochow arsenal. The Yamen after investigating the matter endorsed the recommendations in the Viceroy's document with certain modifications and additions as follows:

According to the original memorial (the Viceroy's) it was stated that, "The establishment of the arsenal dates back thirty years. The money spent amounts to from one to ten millions [taels]. If plans for the reorganization and enlargement of the arsenal are not immediately made then all former work will have been in vain. What a great pity that would be!" We [the members of the Yamen] note that the arsenal was founded by the late Grand Secretary Tso Tsung-t'ang and completed by the former Viceroy of the Liang Kwang provinces Shên Pao-chên. With frugality and painstaking care they conducted the arsenal. Those whom they employed were for the most part poor native scholars dressed in cotton clothes and straw hats . . . who personally took charge of the work entrusted to them, with good results unparalled in other arsenals and factories. . . . Within the past ten or more years Western processes of manufacturing have constantly changed becoming daily more refined. Although the returned students at the Foochow arsenal are well trained and are able to draw plans and construct models, yet because of a lack of funds they can neither add new machines and modernize or enlarge the arsenal, nor can they secure the raw materials necessary for actual construction.

In order to modernize the arsenal the Yamen suggested that ". . . more machines be bought and foreign experts be employed to supervise the work. . . ." Pien's report criticized the practise of sending naval students abroad stating that their ". . . time abroad was too short and at first they accomplished nothing. Their expenses were too heavy for the government to meet. This [practise] is not as good as that of employing [foreign] instructors to come to the arsenal and take charge of courses. . . ." The Yamen, however, did not approve, stating that it would be better to ". . . select [from the two schools at the arsenal—the English school of Navigation and the French school of Naval construction—]

only the more accomplished students to be sent abroad . . ."
as facilities were lacking in China to give them advanced
technical instruction. The reason why the Chinese returned-
student seemed to lack ability was because he was not given
the opportunity properly to employ his special training. The
Yamen suggested that a list of returned students be made
and sent to its office that they might be recommended to the
provincial authorities for responsible positions. The Yamen
also recommended that more money be appropriated to enlarge and modernize the arsenal. It also endorsed the Viceroy's suggestion that a high official be appointed to be resident at the arsenal in full control. This official was to be of
sufficient rank to be able to memorialize the throne in collaboration with the Manchu General-in-Chief of Fukien, the
Viceroy, and the ranking official of the South China or the
North China area. Furthermore, the navy was to be under his
direct control. The Emperor sanctioned the memorial.[8]

Many other petitions of a similar nature appeared in the
years immediately following 1895, aiming to make China a
modern military and naval power. A number of these petitions received imperial sanction. However, in carrying out
these programs, it usually happened that achievement fell far
short of desire.

Of more significance and interest were the steps taken toward the establishment of semi-modern schools in all parts
of the Empire. In 1898 Chang Chih-tung collected a number of the better essays written by students at modern schools
already established in Shanghai, and published them in his
own name under the title of *An Exhortation to Learning*.
The work was given Imperial sanction and widely read
throughout the land, over a million copies being sold, it was

reported.[9] The influence of the book, appearing as it did under the endorsement of one of the foremost officials, was very great. It helped considerably in paving the way for fundamental educational reform after 1900.

In 1896 an official book-translation bureau was established in Peking under Sun Chia-nai, a prominent official, who later was to play a leading rôle in bringing about the abolition of the old examination system. About one thousand taels a month, needed to conduct the bureau, came from the Tsungli Yamen. The memorial requesting its establishment contained a long account of the value of western science; of the development of schools in France, Russia, America, and England; of the number receiving education in those lands and expenses connected therewith. It was also requested that foreigners be added to the staff of the bureau to assist in translating books and newspapers.[10] The modern educational world was gradually being opened up to the Chinese officials.

In June 1896 Ministerial Vice-President Li Tuan-fên presented an interesting memorial thought to have come from the pen of Liang Ch'i-ch'ao. He gave five reasons why he believed so few talented men had come from the modern schools established during the preceding twenty-five years. These reasons were, that students in the *T'ung Wên Kuan* and elsewhere had studied western subjects too much and neglected to consider how to make their own country rich and strong in a practical fashion; that the courses were too general and lacking in technical training save at the Wuhan colleges; that the students did not do actual experimental work, partly, or chiefly because the schools for the most part lacked scientific apparatus, nor were the students going abroad actually to investigate; that the students were too young and that the schools were far too few and the number of students as well. He continued by outlining a system of modern education for China. This was one of the first memorials advocating the adoption of a modern educational system.

In his memorial Li suggested first that a thorough investigation be made of the technical, agricultural, commercial, military, and mining schools abroad, and that books be translated into Chinese. He thought actual experimentation highly important, but because of the expense of apparatus it was necessary that students go abroad for a time to obtain this phase of their education. Within China he advocated the establishment of schools in each province and county and that exceptional youths between the ages of twelve and twenty be selected from among the people to attend them.

He further recommended that the curricula of the prefectural and county schools consist of the *Szu Shu*[11] "Four Books," the *T'ung Chien Kang Mu* "Mirror of History," and the *Hsiao Hsüeh* "Lesser Learning" as a background, to which were to be added foreign languages, literature, arithmetic, astronomy, geography, simple international history, and common easy science. This course was to last three years. Then in the provincial schools students were to be selected below the age of twenty-five years to study the *Wu Ching* "Five Classics,"[12] Chinese history and philosophy, together with science, astronomy, mathematics, manufacturing, silk cultivation, soldiering and mining. This course was also to take three years for completion. From the provincial schools the students were to come to the University which was to be established at Peking. It was for students under thirty years of age and was to have the same curricula as the provincial schools, but with higher standards. He suggested that the old literary name *Shu Yüan* for the provincial colleges be changed to the more literal *Hsüeh T'ang*. The University was to be a model for all others to be established later.

As is appparent there was no plan nor desire to achieve universal education, but rather to train a select number of students. However, Li continued his memorial by outlining a plan for popular education, which was a real innovation in China. To achieve it he suggested the establishment of public libraries in which the poor might read. These libraries were to obtain modern translated books from the *T'ung Wên Kuan,* or Imperial College, at Peking and the arsenal translation bureaus in Shanghai and Foochow. He pointed out that the province of Kiangnan already had three such libraries. In order to supply these libraries and the schools with modern books he recommended that a translation bureau be opened in Peking. In all such bureaus then functioning he emphasized that the books were on science. There should also be more books translated dealing with foreign education, farming, commerce, railroading, and the post office. As science was constantly developing in the West, he concluded that most of the science books then translated were already out of date. The new bureau was to sell the books as cheaply as possible.

Furthermore, he advocated the establishment, in all principal cities of newspaper-translation bureaus to keep the government and all provincial bureaus informed concerning important daily events in the world. In Shanghai and elsewhere he noted that a few newspapers were then being printed. The editors of these he observed, were for the most part poorly educated and their newspapers, consequently, were not to be relied upon. Last of all he suggested that students be sent abroad to study and to investigate. His conclusion as to the reason why his suggested reforms should be carried out reveal him as an ardent patriot. In reform lay the hope of removing the "nation's shame" incurred by the recent defeat at the hands of the Japanese.[18] This program which Li Tuan-fên drew up in collaboration with others was not fully acted upon until 1903, as shall be seen later. However, memorials of a similar nature, following it, led the government to adopt certain phases of his comprehensive plan.

Another significant petition of this period was that presented by Shêng Hsüan-huai, then Director-General of the China Merchants' Steam Navigation Company, as well as of the Imperial Chinese Telegraphs. It also was presented in 1896—and in support of Li Tuan-fên's memorial. Sheng believed that the way to build a strong nation was to train good soldiers, but to train good soldiers plenty of money was necessary. And to have sufficient funds trade and industry must be developed. In order to achieve both ends, talented youths must be trained. In this connection he raised three points. The first dealt with the importance of training soldiers as in western lands, where every man was a soldier and was well paid, a fact which encouraged him to fight. The second point dealt with the importance of increasing the wealth of the country by opening factories and developing commerce. The third point stressed the necessity for training men of talent. He stated that the reason western countries had so many talented men was because farmers, laborers, merchants and soldiers, as well as officials, were educated.

He admitted the impossibility of bringing it all about at once, so suggested that provincial schools be developed first.

He criticized the poor results obtained by the *T'ung Wên Kuan* and the *Kuang Fang Yen Kuan* even though their students did go abroad, because what they learned was not of a practical nature. Mr. Shêng then outlined what he and Liu K'un-i were doing in Shanghai, and made a further suggestion that there be established in Shanghai and Peking two colleges *(Ta Ch'êng Kuan)*. Thirty to forty students should be selected to attend these colleges, and courses in English, French, law, politics, public or international law, and commercial organization and communications should be taught. The students were to be prospective officials for the Foreign Office and for foreign service, and, above all, he thought it most important to separate them from other students trained for practical work within the country. Shêng did not forget, in suggesting these reforms, to pay respect to Confucius and the classics by emphasizing the necessity for instruction in Confucian morality. This petition was favourably received and referred to the Council of State, the Tsungli Yamen and the Board of Finance for consideration.[14]

We see by a memorial presented by the Tsungli Yamen in October 1896 that Li Tuan-fên's memorial concerning enlargement of schools in each metropolitan area, prefecture, and county was granted in part and that the *Shu Yüan* were ordered to add technical courses. The Yamen also approved Shêng's *Ta Ch'êng Kuan* schools and expressed the hope that all provincial officials would establish military schools in their capitals.[15]

Many of the memorials of this period asked permission to enlarge the *Shu Yüan,* or to establish new provincial colleges in which western subjects were to be taught. Even from far Yunnan came such a memorial asking for permission to add sciences and mathematics, and stated that as late as 1880 a *Shu Yüan* was established in which no provision was made for teaching modern subjects.[16]

Another interesting memorial presented early in 1898 by the Tsungli Yamen asked for permission to provide special courses in governmental affairs, finance, modern science, mathematics and military science for officials and others too old to enter schools again, and that yearly they be given the opportunity to take special examinations in these subjects. This memorial was given Imperial sanction.[17]

The problem of translating foreign books into Chinese, in order to hasten the spread of modern knowledge, received considerable attention by the officials in this period, as noted above. In the year 1894 Ma Chien-chung presented a petition on this subject. Ma, who was a great scholar, had spent many years in France. In his petition he stated that China was always being cheated by other countries, hoodwinked, as it were, because the Chinese did not read foreign books and could not understand western conditions or methods. He pointed out that during the Ming dynasty many missionaries translated the classics, biographies, and outlines of Chinese history into Latin, French, and English, while in K'ang Hsi's reign (1662-1723) a Chinese library *(Han Wên Shu Kuan)* was established in Paris. He lamented the fact that in China very few books had been translated, and that most of those had been poorly rendered. He then outlined a plan for the establishment of a translation bureau.[18] It was during this period that Yen Fu—perhaps the most capable and energetic translator of the time—was translating into Chinese such books as Huxley's *Evolution and Ethics,* J. S. Mill's *On*

Liberty and *Logic,* Spencer's *Study of Sociology* and Adam Smith's *Wealth of Nations.*[19]

During this period, 1895-1900, a few modern schools were established—usually at the instigation of an important Viceroy. Frequently this was done in coöperation with foreigners, for the most part missionary-educators, who were conveniently at hand and best fitted for the task. Thus in 1895 Shêng Hsüan-huai presented a memorial to the Superintendent of Trade for the northern ports *(Pei Yang Ta Ch'ên),* Wang Wên-shao, outlining a plan for the establishment of a *Chung Hsi Hsüeh T'ang* which was to form a model for the type of schools appearing after 1900. Wang transmitted the petition in a memorial to the Emperor, on September 30, 1895, requesting that the name of the school be the *Pei Yang Hsi Hsüeh* (North China School of Modern Learning). Two days later a decree sanctioned the memorial. Shêng in his petition stated:

I humbly observe that the best way to strengthen the nation is to educate men of talent. The way to discover men of talent is to first of all establish schools. . . . Japan since the Restoration (1868) has adopted western methods and opened modern schools and colleges (Shu Yüan). Both military and naval officers are selected from among the (graduates) of these schools. From the law schools come (Japan's) foreign representatives together with their staffs. Workers engaged in making guns and ammunition, in working mines and in building roads, come from schools of engineering [with training in] geology and chemistry. Prosperity has thereby been attained within a period of only ten years.

In China there are intelligent people to be found everywhere, but the method of selecting a general is from a multitude of people lacking in special training; the selecting of ministers from those taking examinations in poetry, and on the writing of essays (*Wên Chang*) ; while those selected for industry come from the working classes and lack a knowledge of literature and of mathematics. It is impossible to compare this situation with that obtaining in other countries!

He, therefore, advocated the establishment of schools leading after eight years of common schooling to industrial training in technical schools. He also recommended that the "... American Vice-Consul at Tientsin, Charles D. Tenney ... be appointed to take charge of courses and instruction (*Tsung Chiao Hsi*). ..." The plan which he advocated further provided that the students should not be examined in Chinese literature by the *Pa Ku* method (the stilted eight-legged essay style), but rather tested on their ability to put practical ideas in clear form. This was one of the first attacks made in a memorial presented to the Throne on the old examination system. Shêng referred to the Imperial Decree of 1895 urging the development of schools, the opening of mines, the building of railroads, the construction of a telegraph system, and above all, the training of a modern army as being the prime reason for the drawing up of his memorial.[20] His plan was not completely carried out, however, until after 1900.

In 1897 as we have seen, Shêng Hsüan-huai also memorialized the throne to establish a *Nan Yang Kung Hsüeh,* or South China Public School. It was to be called a public school as half of the money for maintenance was to come from official sources, and half from two semi-private institutions—the China Merchants' Steam Navigation Company, and the Telegraph Company.[21] The work of organizing it was entrusted to Mr. Ho Mei-sun, the first President, and Dr. John C. Ferguson his associate.[22] In an address delivered before the first graduating class, in 1903, Dr. Ferguson said that the original faculty as well as the pupils came from many different provinces, and that the preparatory training of most of the students was quite unequal and very often inadequate. Some of the pupils knew a little English, but had taken no general elementary subjects; while some had only studied translations of rudimentary scientific and mathematical books. All wanted to go through the courses in the shortest possible time. There were no textbooks based on class-room methods of a modern pedagogical nature in Chinese for teaching language, literature and history in the college. So they commenced to prepare these books and were pioneers in this type of work. The President and his associate also established the first normal training school to meet the great need of building up a modern trained teaching staff.[23]

In a newspaper account of the first graduation exercises we note the following: "One of the most interesting features of the programme was the military drill on the campus. The cadets were dressed in neat uniforms of modern cut and performed their evolutions with remarkable precision. A large and well-trained drum and fife corps added to the zest of the drill and presented a natty appearance in brown uniforms and cockaded caps."[24] Dr. Ferguson himself informed the author that the simplest way in which to introduce modern sports in China and to overcome the Chinese students' traditional sedative habits was to provide military drill for them. This they were eager to do being deeply aroused over the defeat of the Empire by the Japanese. The conditions of militaristic aggression under which China was led in desperation to adopt a modern school system made militarism an integral part of it and this *mésalliance* has continued to the present.

At Wuhan, in the fall of 1897, there was established a

modern school with Liang Ch'i-ch'ao as principal. A school newspaper was established *(Hsiang Hsüeh Hsin Pao)* which took on a critical tone quite in keeping with the aggressive and provincially patriotic temper of the Hunanese. A progressive student society *(Nan Hsüeh Hui)* was also organized. After the *coup d'état* in the autumn of 1898 when the Empress-Dowager set aside the Emperor because of his extreme reform measures, the society, as well as the newspaper, was suppressed.[25]

This concludes the survey of the more important developments in thought and practise toward the adoption of modern education up to the time of the Hundred Days Reform from June to September 1898. For a brief period progressive officials and literati under the leadership of K'ang Yu-wei and Liang Ch'i-ch'ao gained the favor of the Emperor and instituted a series of reforms in all spheres of government. Several score of decrees were issued. The more important decrees bearing on education were as follows:[26]

June 23rd—Abolishing the Wenchang essay as a prominent feature in the examinations, this being universally admitted as crippling to Chinese thought.

June 27th—Ministers and princes to report on the adoption of Western arms and drill for the Manchu Banners.

July 4th—Agricultural schools to be established in each province.

July 4th—Indicating an intention to appoint Sun Chia-nai, a progressive, to be president of the new university of Peking.

July 6th—Ministries ordered to report on the substitution of mental tests, in the military examinations, for the existing tests of archery, riding and sword-brandishing.

July 10th—Establishing colleges and schools in all district cities,

> and ordering that all memorial and unofficial temples should be used for the purpose. . . .
>
> July 29th—School boards to be established in every city in the empire. . . .
>
> Aug. 9th—Peking University established; Sun Chia-nai appointed president; Dr. W. A. P. Martin appointed head of the faculty and granted second civil rank (red button). . . .
>
> Aug. 10th—Junglu and Liu K'un-i ordered to consult and report on the establishment of a naval academy and training ships.
>
> Aug. 16th— Government Bureau of Translation established. . . .
>
> Aug. 21st —Schools to be established abroad, under the auspices of the legations, for the sons of Chinese abroad. . . .
>
> Sept. 5th—On the recommendation of Chang Yin-hwan, a beginning to be made in organizing with Western drill a national army based on conscription, involving the abolition of the Green Banner, the "Regular" Chinese army. . . .
>
> Sept. 8th—Decrees on labour relief, the encouragement of machinery (sic), and a medical school. . . .
>
> Sept. 12th—The examinations for military degrees to be remodelled.

The period of the Hundred Days of Reform was followed, upon the return to power of the Empress Dowager, Tz'ŭ-hsi, at the head of the conservatives, by a period of reaction which countenanced the rise of the Boxers in Shantung and their spread through the northern provinces. The foreign concession-hunting during the years 1898-1900 and the threatened dismemberment of the Empire was used by the reactionary officials then in power to direct the fury of the Boxer bands against the westerners. Then followed the mid-summer madness of 1900; the invasion of the capital by the allied troops and the flight of the court to Shensi. Once more the Manchus were humiliated and this time the conservatives were forced by the pressure of public opinion to yield to reform. Even before the Court returned to the capital, decrees were issued that were to lead to fundamental alterations in the educational as well as governmental system.[27]

The first important reform decree issued in January, 1901 ordered all officials at home and abroad, all governmental bureaus, and all ministers in western lands to survey western methods of governing and to report their findings within two months.[28] This decree gave Imperial sanction to reform. All progressives could now come forward with their ideas and plans and present them through the Governors and Viceroys to the Throne. Chang Chih-tung, Viceroy of Hukwang, and Liu K'un-i, Viceroy of Chekiang and Kiangsu, presented at this time a series of three important memorials which formed the basis for subsequent reforming decrees. The first dealt with education; the second with financial, administrative and military reforms; while the third submitted plans by which to select students in considerable numbers to go abroad, to introduce western physical exercises and military drill, to enlarge the number of troops, to improve agriculture and industry, to fix mining regulations, to develop roads and communications, to draw up modern laws, to modernize the coinage of money, to promote postal communications and to translate foreign books. The first memorial was presented in June, 1901. After quoting from the above Imperial Decree the petitioners suggested that the way to make a "Self-strong" (Tzŭ Ch'iang) nation, was to establish modern literary and military schools; change and improve literary examinations; abolish military examinations; and encourage students to go abroad.[29]

As usual the memorialists, in order to win the conservative officials over to reform, resorted to historical argument and searched through China's past in quest of precedents for the proposed change.

In the selection of officials during the time from the Han to the Sui [206 B.C.-590 A.D.] one method was employed and from the T'ang to the Ming [618-1368] another. But both methods whether by selection through election or recommendation [*Hsüan Chü*] or by examinations [*K'ao Shih*] have their faults and their advantages their main purpose was practically the same. From Han and Wei to the Sui dynasty the *Hsüan Chü* method was employed though occasionally the *K'ao Shih* system was resorted to. . . . From T'ang and Sung to the Ming dynasties the *K'ao Shih* method was more in use, though the *Hsüan Chü* system was also employed. . . . However, these two methods only provided means for selecting (officials) from among those already educated. . . . Therefore, private schools provided the courses of study, while the public schools only examined (the students in what they had previously learned). All this was not in accord with the system in vogue during the period of the Three Dynasties [Hsia, Shang and Chou which ruled over China from antiquity to 255 B.C.] The system used at the present time is the one following the regulations of the *K'o Chü* and was copied from the Ming dynasty [1368-1644].[30]

In times of peace there were enough talented men to govern the land and pacify the people, but the country is now overcome by a great catastrophe and sufficient talent is lacking. If we do not change our course how can we save the country from this perilous situation? . . . According to the *Chou Kuan* [a work on the regulations and institutions governing the Chou dynasty 1122-256 B.C.], and also according to the Lesser T'ai's *Li Chi* [the Classic on Ceremonials], the responsibilities and functions of the officer of education [*Szu T'u*] involved the providing of courses in moral training and in professional training as well. . . . Local and national schools as well taught the Six Arts.[31] The prominent official's [*Ta Fu*] responsibilities required that he should possess the nine abilities.[32] Instruction in the reading of literature along with practise in the ceremonies and in fighting was given. . . According to the system of the Three Dynasties graduates of the district schools were called *Shih,* scholars or gentlemen, the soldiers [*Tsu Wu*] were also called *Shih,* thus in reality the soldier and scholar were one. This is [also] clear proof that literary and military training were equally emphasized. For example, Confucius knew both the literary and the military arts, having studied in the four corners of the world. . . .

Later, under the Han dynasty, foreign legates were employed as officials. During the T'ang dynasty Ouigurs[33] were permitted to become officials. The bibliographical section of the Sui dynastic history contains many books dealing with the foreign languages of Central Asia.[34] In the early Ming dynasty the courses [leading to literary degrees] included archery and riding. In K'ang Hsi's time [1662-1723] Westerners [the Jesuit Fathers] were used in making astronomical observations and in manufacturing cannon. The maps of the Imperial Household were drawn by means of the western system of latitude and longitude, while the copper plates from which they were printed employed the Japanese method of *Yin Yang Wên* (incising the character so as to obtain white on black or of cutting the character in relief thus printing black on white). The boundary stone between Russia and China near Nerchinsk [as a result of the treaty of 1689] bears three languages (Chinese, Russian and Latin). During the reign of Ch'ien Lung [1736-1796] there was compiled by Imperial order, in 1763 in 24 ch'üan, the *Hsi Yü T'ung Wên Chih* [or phrase book for the languages of Central Asia including Manchu, Chinese Mongolian, Tibetan and neighboring regions, Tartar and Mohammedan].[35] As to the courses of instruction for the members of the Imperial Household, it is required of those members of the Eight Banners [the Manchu military force] who become officials that they be trained in literary as well as military affairs. The ancient system of our ancestors is really capable of being a model for ten thousand ages!

Today the methods used in the schools of each western country are similar in fundamentals to that of the period of the Three Dynasties—that is, men possessing *Li* [virtue and talent] may be found among the common or uncultivated people. [Following a brief outline of the different types of western schools the memorialists assert], . . . that [the western] regulations governing the promotion or demotion of students through examinations is similar to that which prevailed under the Northern Sung [960-1127] known as the *Chi Fên Shêng Shê*.[36] This method of determining whether the candidate has superior or inferior talents is well founded in reality for there is no danger of the examiner marking according to his prejudice. . . . Therefore, talented men daily increased in number, and the nation flourished constantly. Germany is the most powerful nation today and its school system is the most developed. Japan attained quickly unto prosperity and the number of its schools is the greatest among all eastern countries. This is clear evidence of the value of a flourishing school system.

The memorialists then set forth in considerable detail Japan's system comparing it to western models. Much space was devoted to a description of military training in the West and in Japan. The point was made that all soldiers received the same training as civilians through college. The adoption of this program in China would mean of course the elevation of the soldier to a plane of social equality with the scholar—a preliminary step to the conception of a nation in arms. The memorialists made this one of the chief points, and as a practical measure to attain it, recommended that military drill-grounds be provided, not only for all the proposed middle schools, but for all the primary schools as well. In conclusion they humbly begged ". . . our Emperor to give his utmost consideration to the perilous situation in which the country now finds itself suggesting that the regulations governing the Japanese national school system be quickly discussed in detail, and adopted, thereby strengthening the hearts of the people and steadying the foundations of the nation. All look respectfully to the Throne to carry out these proposals."[37]

The suggestions given in this and other memorials concerning educational reform presented during this period were immediately acted upon. An Imperial decree was issued, August 29, 1901 stating that the old military system obtaining from a time before the Ming, as well as from the Ming dynasty itself, which the Ch'ing took over, was defective because it included only the practises of fencing, archery and horsemanship. It pointed out that these exercises were without value in the training of a modern soldier and should therefore be changed. Accordingly it was ordered that the former military examinations for boys were first to be abolished. Those who had already practiced the old military arts were granted special permission to take for a time the former examinations in order to enter the newly established provincial military schools.[38] On September 11, 1901 the Empress Dowager issued another decree commanding that military schools of the modern type be established throughout the Empire. Moreover, as there were already such schools in Tientsin, Nanking, Wuchang and Tsinan, the Viceroys of those respective areas, Li Hung-chang, Liu K'un-i, Chang Chih-tung and Yüan Shih-k'ai should lose no time in drawing up regulations for them.[39]

Though the Chinese reformed first along military lines, yet within four years the literary as well as military examinations of the old type were abolished. The process, however, was gradual. On August 29, 1901 the Empress Dowager issued a decree, similar in substance to that issued by Kwang Hsü three years earlier, providing for the abolition of the *Wên Chang* or "eight-legged essay" and substituting for it a discussion in essay style of current affairs. The decree also pointed out that as commercial affairs were daily increasing in complexity practical knowledge concerning foreign countries should be taught. It was rather unusual for the Throne even to mention commercial and industrial activities. Apparently the conception of a strong Empire now included not only a modernized army, but also an expanding and thriving commercial and industrial society. Out of this conception was soon to spring, as will be noted below, the idea of the value and importance of promoting a school system which would provide an education for all by the government itself.

The decree ordered that beginning with the following year (1902) the district examinations, the first step on the long trail that led to high political preferment, should examine in five subjects relating to Chinese political history and current affairs; five subjects relating to international politics; and in the ability to expound the *Four Books*. The students were to be examined equally in all three and to use the essay form. Furthermore, candidates presenting themselves for the bachelor degree should be examined in the classics, but a special test should be given in Chinese political history and in international politics.[40]

On September 24, 1901, a decree of great importance was issued which stated that because of the lack of talented men (here again the old Chinese aim of education appears) all should respect the profession of teaching and exhort more students to study. It was planned, therefore, to establish a modern university in Peking, while in each provincial capital the *Shu Yüan,* or Provincial College, was to be made into a modern university modelled after that of Peking. In each *fu, t'ing* and *chihlichou* (administrative units next in importance to the province) middle schools were to be established. In each *chou* and *hsien,* the smallest units, as many primary schools as possible were to be started. In these schools the great principles of the *Four Books* and the *Five Classics* were to be taught as major subjects, while the minor subjects were to be Chinese history, international politics and western science. The aim was to train more talented men so that they might have a realistic grasp of the problems of the day. The regulations governing the examination of students and selecting teachers were to be drawn up by a Central Educational Affairs Bureau to be established and attached to the old *Li Pu* or Bureau of Rites.[41] This decree tried to carry out a program similar in nature to one outlined by Li Tuan-fên five years earlier.[42] The intention of the government autocratically to control all phases of the educational system from the capital was evident from the outset. It was the policy of the Court to centralize all educational reforms and developments which were already underway in the provinces, many of which were launched by the practically autonomous governors and viceroys without Imperial sanction.

A decree was issued September 16, 1901, pointing out that already the provinces of Kiangnan, Hupei and Szechuan had selected students to go abroad to study. The Throne sanctioned this action and encouraged others to do the same.[43] Only students of good moral character were to be chosen and those well versed in Chinese literature. These students were to be given every encouragement and upon their return were to be allowed to take the examinations for the official decrees.

These same regulations were to apply to students who went independently.[44] This decree started the rush abroad and, within a few years, more than 2,000 students were studying in Japan.

On January 10, 1902, Chang Pai-hsi was appointed to take general charge of educational affairs.[45] This appointment was immediately followed by a decree that the *T'ung Wên Kuan,* which was formerly under the Foreign Office, be placed under the control of the newly established university with Chang Pai-hsi at the head. This appointment, which presaged the modern office of Minister of Education, developed normally out of the old administrative system. The rapid growth of the embryonic educational system necessitated at this early date a special bureau. By the end of 1902 there were modern provincial universities in a number of leading provinces.[46] Middle and primary schools also sprang up in rapidly increasing numbers under the incentive and control of provincial authorities.

A more detailed account of the educational developments in two of the provinces will reveal the energy with which the Chinese officials now set about to modernize the Empire and at the same time give an indication of the immediate achievements stemming from the series of memorials and decrees summarized above. In June, 1902 the modern Imperial University of Shansi Province was opened. The history of its founding is an interesting story. Following the Boxer troubles the renowned missionary, Dr. Timothy Richard was asked by the Chinese Plenipotentiaries to aid them in coming to an agreement with the Foreign Powers as to reparations to be made for massacres in the province of Shansi. Dr. Richard, who was noted for his influence among officials, due to his ability to read and write Chinese, had, as early as 1894, conceived of a plan for using some surplus American indemnity money for educational purposes in China.[47] After consulting with other missionaries he proposed, that instead of the Western governments demanding indemnities for the lives of missionaries murdered in Shansi province in 1900, the Chinese government pay annually for ten years the sum of 50,000 taels as a fine, to be used for the founding of a university in the province. Following the adoption of this plan, he was placed in control of the institution for a period of ten years after which it was to revert to the Chinese. Before the idea could be carried out, the Government issued decrees for the establishment of an Imperial university there. When Dr. Richard arrived in Taiyuanfu in 1902, he found work had already begun toward the establishment of this institution. There was no need for two universities, so after "prolonged deliberations" a new contract was drawn for the combining of the two, by which the Chinese authorities were to control all finances and the Chinese department, while Richard was to control the department of Western literature and a translation bureau appended thereto.[48]

As a result of these "long deliberations" a memorial was presented by the provincial governor Tsên Ch'un-hsüan during the year 1902 setting forth the case as outlined above, but expressing opposition as follows:

"At first we thought he [Richard] really cared for Shansi very much, because he wished to use this money to establish a university to cultivate Shansi's talented men, but the formation of the curriculum, the selection of the teachers and the control of the students are all in his hands. It seems to us, therefore, that he invades our educational prerogatives." The

memorialist pointed out that there were no regulations for-
bidding missionaries to establish schools. Therefore, as he
did not wish to cause trouble, he suggested that the two
schools combine with the result seen above.[49]

An account of the development of modern education in
Shansi by 1904 shows a rapidity of development that reveals
an energy and organizing skill unequalled perhaps in educational work. This period of strenuous educational reconstruction lasted until the end of the Empire and continued under
its own momentum in spite of revolution and counter-rev-
olution until about 1918. The development as outlined below
was paralleled in some degree throughout the greater part
of the Empire. By 1904 the Shansi Provincial Education
Bureau, had eighty-one elementary schools established in
as many district cities, and eight middle schools established
in eight prefectural cities. The aid of Japanese advisors was
sought in organizing and constructing the curricula. In primary schools Confucian morals, *Four Books,* Chinese history, geography, arithmetic, composition, and characters and
gymnastics were taught. In the middle schools Confucian
morals, the *Five Classics,* composition, mathematics, history,
geography, foreign languages (English, French or Japanese), drawing, general science, physics, chemistry and gymnastics were taught. At that time normal schools had not been
opened. The following colleges were at Taiyuan, the provincial capital: an agricultural college of 100 students with two
Japanese professors of agriculture and forestry; a Manchu
college for Manchus only; a college for expectant officials
who were to be examined once a month in government and
law. There was a military college of 120 students and eight
instructors, and a police training institute with two Japanese

instructors. All this had developed within four years in a province of 8,000,000 inhabitants.[50]

In Hunan there also was rapid development. When the government decreed that the temples be made into schools much active opposition was aroused through the instigation of the priests. Threats were made against officials and foreigners. However, the officials maintained a firm hand, explained the purpose of the decree and resentment quickly died down. By 1905 there were modern school buildings in almost every prefectural city and temples were rapidly being restored to the priests. Public reading rooms were being opened. Japanese instructors were to be found in most of the schools. Military drill was being conducted in Japanese fashion under the guidance of these instructors.[51]

In spite of all this activity, it was soon realized that, unless the literary examinations were abolished, students would not go to the new type of schools in any great number, for the conception that education was only a means to enter official circles, with all the attendant social honor and wealth which that achievement might mean, could not be effaced in a day, nor a year, nor even in a generation.[52] Yüan Shih-k'ai, then Viceroy of Chihli, and Chang Chih-tung, then Viceroy of the Liang Kwang presented a joint memorial to the throne in February, 1903 in which they pointed out how weak China was, being daily cheated and deceived by the western nations. It was time, they stated, that China awaken. Capable men were needed, they said, and they could be obtained only through education. They emphasized the point that Japan and western countries had many schools, military as well as literary; that all children from seven to thirteen years of age in those countries must go to school or the parents would be punished. These countries had both private and public schools and all helped to support them. Each student was trained according to his ability. This was the way to strengthen the nation. The memorial asked that the Empress Dowager continue to urge the provinces to establish more schools. So far not enough money had been forthcoming to support the schools, the chief obstacle being the literary examinations. The old *Wên Chang* was of no value in discovering the real ability of students. The national government should be responsible for higher education and the people for the common schools, but because of the desire to educate only for official life the people would not collect money to establish schools that aimed at a broad, general education. Thus China's very existence depended upon the abolition of the literary examinations and the establishment of a flourishing school system that aimed to cultivate the individual's real ability. The memorial in conclusion asked for the gradual abolition of the old examination system.[53]

Apparently no action had been taken by the government regarding the foregoing petition as another one was presented, written in a similar vein, with a plan for the gradual abolition of the old literary examinations. It was presented by Chang Pai-hsi, Yung Ch'ing and Chang Chih-tung in 1903. They again pointed out that money would not be forthcoming from the people for the establishment of schools as long as the literary examinations existed.[54]

The above two memorials were not sufficient to move the government, whereupon Yüan Shih-k'ai, Viceroy of Chihli, General Chao Erh-hsün, Chang Chih-tung, Viceroy of the Hu provinces, Chou Fu, Viceroy of the Kiang provinces, Ts'ên Ch'un-hsüan, Viceroy of the Kwang provinces and

Tuan Fang, Governor of Hunan presented a vigorous memorial demanding the immediate abolition of the examinations. It was presented August 21, 1905, just after the close of the war between Russia and Japan. The petitioners pointed out, that during recent years each nation wanted China to revive and change its system. One notes, time and again, how keenly aware the Chinese were of foreign criticism and attitudes and were influenced accordingly. The tenor of the memorial ran as follows: The Russo-Japanese treaty of peace is about to be concluded and we are in greater danger than ever. We must arise and show the world that we are not conservative. The foreigners all point out to us the evil of our examination system.[55] If we change, they will open their eyes in amazement. Students who have studied only in China emphasize study for sake of study. On the other hand those who have returned from study abroad have caught the foreign idea of the function of the school as a preparation for life and do not strive simply to pass examinations.

The main aim in establishing schools is not only to select men of talent, but also to awaken the intelligence of the common people and develop universal education. On the one hand they can be faithful to the nation and on the other be true to their own individuality. The more highly talented men can directly serve their country and the others will make better and more useful members of the nation.
Soldiers, farmers, workers, and business men all have their respective duties and work. Women and girls have their education in performing duties about the home. Schools everywhere and everyone studying will make China rich and strong. It was in this way that Prussia defeated France, and Japan, Russia.

But the great obstacle was the literary examinations. Many people opposed their abolition for fear that the classics might be neglected. This the memorialists pointed out was untrue as, in schools then running according to modernized curricula, the classics held the most important place. The defect of the old examination system was, that it did not test the morality and character of applicants, whereas the new school curricula devoted whole courses to character training.[56]

In pursuance of this urgent memorial the Throne, on September 2, 1905, issued a decree abolishing the lower examinations at once and the higher from the beginning of 1906. The Throne recognized that the strength of Japan and the western nations lay in their school systems and in the study of science. The Viceroys and Governors were ordered to establish new schools as rapidly as possible, that the people might be privileged to attend. In the new system the study of the classics and textbooks on ethics were to be the foundation of the curriculum. All the people, merchants as well as farmers, were admonished to appreciate the value of universal education, for not only would the nation profit by it, but each class shine in the glory of it. Schools, therefore, were to be established as rapidly as possible and textbooks were to be chosen so that the people might know what to study and a uniform system of education be inaugurated.[57]

In keeping with the primary aim to strengthen the nation, another decree followed this one a month later, urging civil officials to send their younger brothers and sons to the modern military schools. The memorial calling it forth emanated from the Board of Military Affairs.[58] The idea of a nation in arms was slowly becoming fixed, though the old civil officials were still opposed instinctively to the degrading profession of arms.

The competitive civil service examinations were abolished

by decree because, as we have seen, they were an obstacle to the development of a modern system of education. This action was the recognition on the part of the more progressive officials, that a nationally and politically controlled system of education, modelled after those in the West and especially after that of Japan, was the most powerful instrument for the strengthening of the nation. The new day demanded more than a mere handful of officials selected on the old basis and having only a general classical training. By this time it was realized that not only modern military and naval officers were needed, but also scientists and industrialists, as well as professional men. For the education of more talented men of a great variety of accomplishments a modern system of education was essential as possessing varied types of schools and curricula. However, the danger was that such a large system would get beyond control of the central authorities and every effort and every means was employed to centralize all educational activities under the Ministry of Education which was presently to be established.

The first modern school system was originally outlined in 1903 by a special commission, consisting of Sun Chia-nai, Chang Pai-hsi and Chang Chih-tung. The findings of the commission were published in a four-volume work, and contained plans for the organization and establishment of the new school system as well as the curricula to be adopted.[59] It was practically an exact copy of Japan's educational system of the time.[60] "The aim of the lower primary school is to give to children about seven years of age the knowledge necessary for life, to establish in them the foundation of morality and patriotism and to promote their physical welfare."[61] Over one-third of the time was to be devoted to the study of Chinese classics and language, the rest to morals or ethics, Chinese history and geography, nature study, physical culture and mathematics. The aim and curriculum of the higher primary schools were practically the same. It was to take nine years to complete the primary school, five years in the lower and four in the higher primary. The middle schools aimed to provide a ". . . higher general education for children between the ages of fifteen and nineteen, so as to prepare them to enter political and industrial life, or the various higher institutions of learning."[62] One-third of the time was to be employed in the study of the classics and Chinese language. Foreign languages were to be taught along with some foreign as well as Chinese geography, history and economics, also the sciences of biology, physics and chemistry.

Among the reasons for the dominating influence of the Japanese system in this formative period of education in China, was the miraculous success Japan was having in the adoption of western sciences and techniques. Her educational system was modelled in many important respects after that of Imperial Germany, though American and French influences were also in evidence. We have noted above that even as early as 1865 certain Chinese officials were looking to Japan as a model.[63] Other factors were the similarity in political and traditional institutions, the proximity to China, and the ease with which the Chinese can learn to read Japanese as compared with western languages. After 1895 Japanese educational influence developed rapidly and by 1904 there were in China, some 165 Japanese teachers, more or less capable and well trained. On the other hand, by 1905 as many as 2,500 Chinese students were in Japan and the number continued to increase rapidly. The majority of these were in normal, military, and law schools. They came from every province in China. Another main source of influence was the translation of Japanese literature into Chinese. One Japanese publishing firm in Shanghai, the *Hsin Min I Yin Shu Chü,* listed 608 works in its catalog for 1904-1905. Of this number 97 were on education, 121 on history, 40 on biography, 43 on geography, 31 on physiology, 27 on political economy, 20 on law, 19 on arts and sciences, 28 on philosophy, 16 on military history, 41 were general essays, 64 poetry and poetical works, and 30 atlases and charts.[64]

Further evidence of the great amount of educational literature appearing at this formative period of modern education in China is seen in a report on the subject, by Dr. Gilbert Reid, at the fifth meeting of the Chinese Educational Association (a Protestant missionary organization) in 1905. He pointed out that at the time there were 680 volumes in Chinese relating to modern education. The Commercial Press, established just at the close of the nineteenth century, by 1905 was publishing sixty different textbooks in the Chinese language, besides some fifty other kinds of books bearing on education. Over one million copies were sold each year. Of this large number of works the Protestant mission presses contributed only sixty-one. In view of the fact that during the last three decades of the nineteenth century a few missionaries were active pioneers in the field of modern education in China his conclusion is all the more significant. He wrote, "Needless to say the educational needs of the Chinese are not being met by this Association. It is really only a small factor."[65]

Not only books, but educational newspapers and magazines commenced to appear at this time. Fully a score or more were being published.[66] One of them, *The Educational World,* first appeared in Shanghai in May, 1901 with Lo Chên-yü as publisher and Wang Kuo-wei as editor. These gentlemen became two of China's foremost scholars in recent times. Their magazine carried many articles bearing on the problem of introducing western education into China. Many of the articles were translations from Japanese educational magazines. A most valuable piece of work was done in the translation of the regulations issued by the Japanese government covering all phases of the educational development in that country. These translations appeared not only in the magazine, but also in a large ten volume special collection *(Chiao Yü Ts'ung Shu Ch'u Chi)* published by these two men. This invaluable compilation was no doubt in the hands of the three officials who in 1903 outlined China's first modern educational system and thus accounts in large measure for the close imitation of the Japanese system.[67]

In view of the high regard in which Lo Chên-yü is held by Chinese scholars, a summary of one of his articles in *The Educational World* appearing in September, 1901, and called "Five Educational Requirements," will be of interest. The first requirement was the necessity of translating foreign books on education. The second urged the retention of the national language, the national literature and the national religion (Confucianism) for the foundation of the educational curricula. The question was asked: "How can a nation exist without its own language and literature?" A warning against the tendency to over-emphasize foreign languages in middle schools was given. They should be used only for scientific and technical courses or courses bearing on international affairs. Always the native language and literature should be dominant. This no doubt was a reaction to missionary school curricula which overemphasized, from the Chinese viewpoint, foreign languages, particularly English. The third point asserted that the educational prerogatives should not be relinquished to foreigners. Lo deplored the tendency of his time to ask foreigners to run the newly established modern educational institutions. Here was an early shot fired in the struggle to "Recover the Educational Prerogatives," a movement culminating twenty years later. The fourth point concerned itself with the necessity for having a full-rounded curriculum, not merely emphasizing western science and languages. The fifth point asserted that the course on ethics was the most important in the curriculum. He pointed out that there were two kinds of morality: individual morality and public morality. Of the two the latter was the more important and for that reason the course on ethics should be given a place of prime importance.[68]

Another article in this same magazine called "China's Education Revolution," though written by the editor of a Japanese educational magazine, not only clearly reflected the attitude of the Japanese toward modern education and what it should consist of, but also gave the prevailing temper and attitude of the more progressive Chinese officials and literati. The prosperity or the decline of a nation, it stated, was based on the number of trained men of ability in the nation, and that in turn depended on its educational system. The reason, for example, why Germany could conquer France, in 1871, was because Germany's educational system was better than that of France. The author stated that he had recently made a trip to China and was struck by the educational changes taking place there. He was glad to see this. Since both China and Japan belong to the yellow race they must together face the western world in order to win equality. He suggested, therefore, the following points as the way in which China might develop a good educational system and a strong nation: The courses on morality should emphasize the teachings of Confucius; the "eight-legged essays" should be abolished; primary and middle schools should use only those textbooks approved by the Ministry of Education; science and mathematics should be emphasized; physical exercise should be encouraged; the students should be encouraged to study foreign books and the Japanese language should be learned, as China and Japan are neighbors; in the primary school all courses should be in the national language, but in the middle and higher schools Japanese should be required and English made elective; religious teaching, whether Buddhist, Catholic or Protestant should be prohibited in the schools, and finally the spirit of patriotism should be encouraged. The difficulty in China, he added, lay in the fact that the family was placed before the nation. Therefore, children should be taught to place the nation before the family.[69]

Another scholar of outstanding importance, who was very influential in popularizing and adapting modern education for the Chinese, was Liang Ch'i-ch'ao. Since the nineties he had been closely associated with the newer educational tendencies. He coöperated as we have seen, with K'ang Yu-wei and others in the reform period of 1898. Following the overthrow of the Emperor, he fled to Japan, where he turned to his favorite profession of journalism, establishing among other papers, the *Hsin Min Pao* ("The New People"). In its pages there appeared innumerable articles, the product of his facile pen, in which were discussed all phases of human activity, with emphasis on the political, interpreting to the thousands of Chinese who flocked to the Island Empire, western arts, government, law, history and education.[70] W. W. Yen, the renowned Chinese diplomat, wrote of him in 1905 as follows:

No other personage has infused such an intense pro-Japanese spirit among the younger men and women of China than has this wonderful reformer and writer, who in a few years has revolutionized Chinese thought and style of composition. Whether the success of his writing be only ephemeral or not, there can be no doubt that, to him, the greatest credit is due for awakening the people of his country to realize the awful danger the country is in, and for opening the eyes of the people to the necessity for reform.[71]

Liang's articles on education were many and varied. He favoured Confucianism for its moral influence, but opposed education by Buddhists and Christians.[72]

Liang Ch'i-ch'ao's address to the students on the occasion of the opening of the modern Hunan school in 1897 revealed the temper of this progressive young reformer's thought at this time. After quoting extensively from the classics he said, "Now you gentlemen, who wear the scholar's robes, and read the writings of the sages, must find out whose fault it is that our country has become so crippled, our race so weak, our teaching so feeble. Is it not because not any one among the four hundred million of people (sic) has taken the responsibility that we have come to this pass?" Then again, he tells them they ought to feel the exhilaration of coming to the help of the nation and to use their minds to alleviate the sorrow of the people. In their study they should read western literature in order to save the nation from the western powers who are " . . . pressing on every hand." The necessity for getting rid of the heavy classical literary style was universally felt among all reformers at this time. Liang tells the students that the aim in composition should be not to get an ornate style. "It is sufficient if the *written discourse* (italics mine) which is intended to awaken or teach the world, meet the demand expressed in the words: 'In language it is simply required that it convey the meaning.' In writing this kind of literature, the principles should be broadly and clearly stated and the style crisp and perspicuous, but need not be embellished." He did not, however, reject the literary style in his own writings at this time.

He continued by deploring the decay of Confucianism and stated that ". . . the central theme in founding schools now should be to take Confucius as the model." He ended with the fervid plea that Confucius may be ". . . again regarded as the example and model of ten thousand ages and the pattern of the world." He urged upon the students to take the vow to spread universal peace and brotherhood throughout the world.[73]

However, Liang's later writings became more racially and nationalistically self-conscious. Moreover, the broader Confucian ideal as stated above was to find an increasingly less important place in the writings of educators as time went on. The Reverend John Darroch, in an article on the state of literature in China about 1905, concluded, after a survey of the newspapers of that time that "The general drift is towards patriotism, progress and righteousness as far as the editors and contributors of the articles see it."[74]

The spirit and attitude of officials toward modern education at this time was clearly revealed in a book written by Kao Pu-ying and Ch'ên Pao-ch'üan called, "What the people should read."[75] It was endorsed by Yüan Shih-k'ai and issued by the Board of Education of the province of Chihli. One hundred thousand copies were printed in the first edition. It was to be distributed among the students of the province. The authors had previously spent a year in Japan, as the content of the book indicates. The first chapter dealt with the relationship between the dynasty, or state, and the people. The point stressed was that the dynasty and the people were one. The habit of saying when the state got into difficulty, "This is the state's affair; it has nothing to do with us," was deplored. For is not, the authors continued, "The distress of the state, the distress of the people?" The example of the Jews, as a people without a state, was given as a warning. The second chapter argued that, because the state gave the people all its benefits, they should be willing to sacrifice their lives as do the soldiers of Germany or Japan; and the third asserted that the protection of the nation was the protection of the people.

The promotion of education as the means of developing a strong nation was the theme of the next chapter. It stated that Bismarck attributed the victory over France to compulsory education. Other nations, including Japan, had followed the Prussian example and China was urged to do the same. In conclusion the authors said ". . . from these facts it can be seen that China's greatest need at the present time is education; once the people become intelligent (sic) they will with united hearts give themselves to the help of their country, and the state will then become strong."[76] The fifth chapter plead for the realization of universal education as a necessity in a world of wild beasts (the states) sharpening their claws to tear each other's flesh. In Japan the fundamental idea of education was militarism. The authors pointed out that the textbooks were filled with tales of war heroes, while patriotism and loyalty to the Emperor underlay all. Even in peace-loving America the same strength was gained through patriotic songs, hence, the recent victory over Spain. Two chapters were devoted to the advocacy of universal conscription and military training, that China might take its proper place among the nations: this was called "armed peace." The example of Japan and Prussia was held forth. China's military spirit and prowess in ancient times were likened to Japan's of today. The problem was to revive it. The eighth chapter lamented China's weakness. Then followed three chapters dilating upon the strength and preparedness of other nations. The final chapter concluded with methods as to how the people of China could save their nation. In the first place in order that there might be peace among the classes, social and official distinctions should be disregarded, for all were sons of the state. The people were admonished not to place too high a value on life; they must be brave soldiers and ready to sacrifice all for the dynasty; they should not be lazy. Each should develop his own trade or industry, thereby would the state become strong. And finally they should not covet wealth. It was better to give some money for the schools of the community than to waste it all on a profligate son. "If these four methods are followed out in all sincerity we will have unity, military power and prosperity."[77]

The great and pervasive influence that one nation has upon

another is here clearly revealed. Also striking is the self-conscious methods adopted by ardent patriots artificially to revive among a people a supposed former military ardor. The artful methods employed by these reforming officials, and their supporters, to militarize the Chinese people is a tribute to their intellectual acumen, however much one may deplore the evil effects of that policy easily apparent in the China of today.

With the administrative reorganization of the Imperial Government, following more or less closely the autocratic examples of Japan and Germany, it was decided, in December 1905, to create a *Hsüeh Pu* or Ministry of Education to be placed on a plane of equality with the other ministries. The prevailing conception of education as a means for the nation to strengthen itself to face a world of warring states, led naturally to the organizational forms of highly centralized autocratic control. The new Ministry of course grew naturally out of previous administrative forms. The memorial that recommended the change was drawn up jointly by the Bureau of Government Affairs, *Chêng Wu Ch'u*[78] and the Committee of Educational Affairs, *Hsüeh Wu Ch'u.*[79] As a result of the decree endorsing the memorial, this Department of Education was taken from under the control of the centuries-old Ministry of Rites and made an independent and equal ministry with the others. By the same decree the ancient *Kuo Tzŭ Chien,* or National College,[80] was amalgamated with the new ministry. Yung Ch'ing, the Chancellor of the Hanlin Academy, the highest educational institution in the Empire, was made the first Minister of Education.[81]

In theory, and to a large degree in practise, the new Ministry had ". . . almost absolute control over the educational system."[82] It was so constituted that it could issue all regulations concerning the establishment of schools, the curricula followed and the textbooks used. It had power ". . . to remove from office any educational officers found inefficient, [to] nominate provincial commissioners of education, and, in short, [it] had absolute control [on paper] of all educational matters in the country . . ." with the exception of certain technical and military schools that were directly under the control of other central authorities.[83] Very little room was left, in theory, for local and provincial initiative. This educational policy was quite in line with the general centralization policy of the government after 1900.

Since the close of Ch'ien Lung's reign at the end of the eighteenth century there had been an increasing amount of decentralization within the Empire. Especially after the T'ai-p'ing rebellion, in the middle of the nineteenth century had the power of the viceroys and governors increased to the point of practical autonomy. Men like Li Hung-chang, Tsêng Kuo-fan, Liu K'un-i, Chang Chih-tung and Yüan Shih-k'ai were practically autonomous feudal lords in their respective provinces. It was under their direct initiative and sanction that educational reforms, as well as all other reforms, commenced to take place. The central authorities would simply, after due time, give to their activities the Imperial sanction of a decree. Thus, as we have already seen, the actual beginnings of a national system of education developed first in Shantung, Chihli, Shansi, Hunan, Kwangtung and Chekiang, where enlightened viceroys and governors held sway.

The newly established Ministry built upon the systems already existing in these provinces, attempting to unify them and extend them throughout the Empire. As long as the Em-

pire lasted and for the first few years of the Republican régime, until the death of Yüan Shih-k'ai in 1916, there was a
certain amount of authority exerted throughout the Empire
by the Minister of Education. Since that time, however, with
the breakdown of the central authority, actual educational
control has fallen into the hands of Educational Associations
and the Provincial Governments. Not all to be sure, but sufficiently so that there was a certain degree of freedom from
bureaucratic control and a consequent flourishing of experimental schools resulting in a diversity of types of schools as
well as of curricula. The Ministry of Education continued to
function throughout the whole of the period from 1905 to
the present, issuing an endless number of decrees, instructions and orders, holding conferences, inspecting and approv-
ing textbooks. Its power and authority varied from time to
time and from province to province; never absolute anywhere, extending from a high degree of control in the northern provinces near the capital to practically no control in the
Yangtze valley provinces and those to the south, especially in
the provinces of Chekiang, Kiangsu and Kwangtung, as well
as in the northern province of Shansi. It is interesting to note
that these very provinces have the most developed educational
systems and have been most successful in adjusting western
educational methods and aims to the Chinese *milieu*.

However, throughout the period, no matter how decentralized and disorganized the political government was, there has
been a striking unity among educators. Educational conferences of a really national character were held and a consistent
harmony of aims and purposes was maintained. At least in
this realm of ultimate aim there was national unity. Not only
in the aim, but also in the curricula adopted and in the text-

books used, this dominant motive of creating a self-conscious Chinese public, aware of its political position in the world, and of its responsibility to better that position through militarization and the creation of a sense of duty on the part of all toward the nation, can be more and more clearly traced. However often the school system was changed, some four times in all, whatever the pedagogical and technical develop ments, this one aim remained dominant.

When in 1903 Chang Chih-tung and his associates presented the plan for the first modern educational system of China, they failed to state its aims with sufficient force or clarity.[84] This resulted in considerable criticism which led the Ministry of Education to present a memorial in March 1906, within three months after it was established, fixing the educational aims. A month later an Imperial decree gave sanction to the substance of this memorial. The memorialists pointed out in the beginning the lack of detail in the report of the Educational Commission of 1903. The Ministry wished to rectify this. The substance of the memorial may be summarized as follows: If the educational systems of Japan and western countries are examined, it will be seen that there are two kinds: technical education and common-school, or popular, education. The latter form is especially emphasized in these countries. The aim is not to educate a talented few (which reformers up to that time had held it primarily to be), but to educate the people of the nation. Now it is necessary that China emphasize popular education and order all to go to school. It is therefore, very important that first of all the aims be stated. These are: loyalty to the throne; respect for Confucius; the awakening of the people to a sense of their national responsibility; the promotion of militarism and the development of reality and practicality in education.

Concerning the first of these aims we note that in recent times Chinese scholars tend to imitate the externals of western governments and to forsake their own nation's monarchical forms. Now the governments of all the countries are not the same, but they are one in that they respect the head of the nation and this is the basis of the nation's strength. Both Germany and Japan respect monarchs as heads of their governments. In Germany the educational system aims to unify the Empire, while in Japan it aims to maintain in direct line the Imperial family for ten thousand generations. In the primary textbooks of Japan there is much space devoted to the teaching of what constitutes the security of the nation. Thus all the children have the idea of striving to erase the nation's shame, while the leaders and the nobility identify their own glory or shame with that of the nation. That is what is called monarch and people being one in body. Some Chinese scholars at present misinterpret the West, saying that westerners always desert the old and embrace the new. They tend, therefore, to desert what is old in China and to disobey governmental regulations. The value of educating the people to be loyal to the Throne is, therefore, of first importance.

Secondly, in each country the educational system aims to respect and preserve the national language, literature, history, customs and religion. Therefore, ceremonies are held to respect the national religion. Now the doctrines of Confucius are most worthy and should become not only China's religion, but also that of the whole world. In the schools the classics must be required and Confucius' birthday must be honored with ceremonies and appropriate music. In this way Confucianism will become the basis of the educational system.[85]

Thirdly, a strong state depends not upon a few heroes, but upon the coöperation of a loyal people and this comes about only through education. Patriotism must be inculcated among the youth as well as the moral cultivation of the individual as taught by Confucius. At present, the Chinese people are selfish and divided. The people of one province, district, village or even family do not recognize or know the other. In order to rise out of this condition the textbooks must emphasize public morality and duty. Moral education consists in creating a sense of public duty that all may treat others as themselves and love their country as they do their families.

Fourthly, what is meant by emphasizing military education? In Japan and in the countries of the West everyone is a potential soldier and must go to the battlefield in time of war. They hold death on the battlefield to be a form of glory. This is brought about by the schools of these countries cultivating among the youth a knowledge of military affairs thus arousing the spirit of militarism. It is true that at the present time our dynasty does emphasize military training as being of the utmost importance, but in order to carry it out the textbooks of the middle and primary schools must be filled with accounts of military affairs, that the idea of militarism may spread among the people. The textbooks of literature, history and geography should clearly recount naval and army battles and illustrate them with pictures of modern military equipment. The course in music should emphasize military songs. The course in physical education should be designed to develop the children's physique. The younger students should be taught to play games and the older ones to do physical exercises in the form of military drill. This will teach them to preserve order, maintain their dignity and thus develop a perfected personality.

Fifthly, what do we mean by emphasizing reality in education? The most valuable result to derive from education is the ability to put to practical use what one has learned. We note that in the West, three hundred years ago, the scholars lost themselves in vague theories and unrealities much the same as most Chinese scholars do today. But since the time of Bacon, an Englishman who developed the theory of experimentalism and demanded proof for all things, western statesmen and educationalists alike have followed what he said. That is why western science and industry are so developed and so progressive at the present time. The textbooks in the Chinese schools should hereafter place less emphasis on theory and more on facts. Scientific research, drawing and handwork should be added to the curricula in order to fit the children for industrial pursuits.

After pointing out the danger of the new school system becoming a mere means for attaining official position, the memorial closed with the hope that the Throne would announce these aims to the whole Empire, especially that the book publishers may know of them and compose their middle and primary school textbooks accordingly. It should also be decreed that these textbooks be submitted to the Ministry for its approval.[86]

An examination of the curricula drawn up on the basis of these aims will throw further light on the spirit of education in the years just prior to the overthrow of the dynasty.

The lower primary school courses covered a period of five years. Eight courses were to be taught uniformly throughout the five years with a total of thirty hours a week. Two hours a week were to be devoted to ethics, twelve to Chinese classics, four to Chinese literature, six to mathematics, one to history, one to geography, one to science, and three to drill. It will be noted that history was given only one hour a week and consisted entirely in reading short stories and the biographies of famous men in Chinese history. Neither the geography nor the history course dealt with the world at large. The geography course covered only China and bordering countries. The drill consisted of physical exercise. In 1909 a change was made in this curriculum reducing the number of subjects. It was decreed that history, geography and the natural sciences were not to be taught as separate courses, but a general knowledge of them was to be introduced into the new readers.[87]

The nine subjects taught during the four years of higher primary school were: morals, two hours; Chinese literature, eight hours; Chinese classics, twelve hours; mathematics, three hours; science two hours; Chinese history, two hours; geography, two hours; drawing, two hours; and physical drill, two hours. In the higher as well as the lower primary school no history of countries other than China was given. In geography foreign countries were treated in a general way. The aim of the course on morals was to develop character through the example of the actions and sayings of great men.[88] In the middle schools a foreign language, usually English or Japanese was to be studied together with the history of the world.[89] However, as only about 5 per cent of those finishing either lower or higher primary school go on to middle school, it may be concluded that 95 per cent of the children educated in China at that time (and China was not unique among nations in that respect) were taught practically nothing concerning the world at large unless the teacher on his own initiative undertook to do so.[90]

Throughout this period from 1895 to 1911 when so much time and energy were devoted to the establishment of a modern system of education, the earlier ideal of education as a means to militarize and strengthen the nation was by no means overlooked. Modern military and naval academies continued to be established. The result of it was that " . . . we find a nation," writes Henry B. Graybill, Acting President of Canton Christian College in 1911, "once opposed to physical education and distinguishing the student from the soldier as the official from the coolie, now making a new class of soldier-students for the defense and glory of the nation, and that chiefly at the expense of the people." Japanese military instructors continued to pour into the country to assist the Chinese to prepare to fight—whom? Japan, no doubt, and each other. Thus by 1911 it was estimated that in the modern armies of China there were over 240,000 soldiers of whom ". . . some 85,000 are properly organized and officered." Mr. Graybill goes on to comment on this as follows: "In spite of the still existing corruption, desertions, vindictive punishments, and love of parade, there is an increasing martial spirit in the army and among the people generally."[91] He writes further:

The effect of this movement for strengthening the forces of the Empire is a part of the general movement for a better standing as a member of the world family of peoples. Thus it is closely connected with the birth of the new school system. *The same spirit is in both and they react upon each other.* (Author's italics.) The social standing of the soldier is raised. He begins to have patriotic emotions and to take pride in his position of importance. The schools on their part have taken on the military air. There are organizations and drill, marching through the streets with fife and drum, uniforms, guns, swords and flags, military drill and gymnastics are given even in the elementary schools. Physical education has suddenly become very popular. At Cheefoo an athletic meet and drill contest were held together last year (1910). . . . Patriotic songs in chorus are frequently heard. Professor O. D. Wannamaker has kindly translated the most popular one at Canton. It is given here in full ·

The yellow dragon signals flying, China's banner gay;
Ten myriad swords flash light athwart the breasts
     that burn to slay;
New songs of war accompany our army marching
     forth;
Behold amid the war clouds their terrible array!
Our ninefold land is filled with fumes of foreign war
     and woe,
Our people chant their battle-songs today against the
     foe
The soldier's blood of sacrifice is daily flowing free;
Forsake not now the liberty beloved from of yore!
With guns upon right shoulder, and with belted knife
     at side,
We desert the royal audience, the decree goes far and
     wide;
Father, mother, wife and children march beside to bid
     farewell
Encouraging their soldiers with jests as on they ride![92]

What price glory? The modern army today numbering between one and two million has done little to better China's international position, but has done incalculable harm to the cause of order and security within the country and brought death and suffering through famine and robbery to tens of millions of Chinese.

By way of summary; the sixteen years, from the close of the war with Japan to the overthrow of the dynasty, saw the abolition of the old examination system and the establishment of a modern system of education under the centralized control of a Ministry of Education at Peking. The prime incentive bringing about this educational revolution lay in the realization on the part of the progressive officials, whose number augmented almost daily, that the very preservation of the state as a political entity depended upon it. Militarism resting on a prosperous commercial and industrial society was conceived to be the means. For the old Confucian ideal of government by virtue was to be substituted the modern ideal of government by law and by technical or specialized skill. Yet in the abolition of the examination system one of the strongest cohesive forces of China's many centuries was lost. The old examinations served as the recruiting agency for the personnel of the administrative system from among the men of talent *(Jên Ts'ai)*. The wealth and prestige accompanying official position was sufficient incentive to cause tens of thousands to study for the examinations, many times the number who would find reward in the limited positions available. The long and arduous path to official position moulded those who failed as well as those who succeeded in the same Confucian principles and virtues. The value of this was clearly seen by the reforming officials, and in the first educational system Confucian teachings were to form the basis of education. However, as will be noted below, Confucianism was completely swept out of the school system after 1916 and for it was substituted modern nationalism.

The abolition of the examination system has proved to be a far more radical measure than even the most far-sighted officials of that time conceived it to be. It dealt the death-blow to Confucianism. Yüan Shih-k'ai, who, as we have seen, played a prominent rôle in the system's annulment, made a futile effort while President of the Republic, 1912-1916, to retain Confucianism as the basis of education. The sudden abolition of the system left many thousands of scholars, who had been preparing for many years to take the examinations, in the lurch. They formed a large discontented class easily subject to the radical ideas pouring in from the West. There being a premium on "western learning" they flocked in large number to Japan and, in smaller number, to western countries where they received a smattering knowledge of western ways and institutions. Upon their return to China they boldly attempted to apply their new knowledge with little understanding or adaptation to Chinese conditions. It is the emergence of this new type of leadership poorly trained in both Chinese and western learning and yet undertaking to transform radically the time-honored traditions of Chinese society that accounts in a large degree for the serious disorganization that marks this period of adjustment to the West. In the hands of this new type of official, the newly launched educational system underwent many vicissitudes as the succeeding chapters will show. Especially interesting to follow, in this respect, is the attempt of Chinese politicians and educators to find in modern nationalism a substitute for the cohesive force of Confucianism and to use the educational system as the medium for instilling nationalist philosophy and sentiments into the hearts and minds of Chinese boys and girls.

Chapter III

MODERN EDUCATION AFTER THE ESTABLISH-
MENT OF THE REPUBLIC

The political revolution commenced in October, 1911. By the beginning of the next year a Republican form of government had been established at Nanking with Sun Yat-sen as the provisional president. He was succeeded in February, 1912 by President Yüan Shih-k'ai. In the early part of 1912 the Ministry of Education was reorganized and called the *Chiao Yü Pu* instead of *Hsüeh Pu* thus emphasizing its educational character more than formerly. Ts'ai Yüan-p'ei, a returned student from Germany and France, was made the first Minister of Education.

The organization of the Ministry differed little from that under the Empire. It aimed to bring all activities of an educational and even quasi-educational nature under its control.[1] A perusal of the *Chiao Yü Kung Pao,* its official periodical, reveals repeated regulations covering all phases of educational activity from primary schools to universities, public lectures, public reading rooms, financial matters, appointment of teachers, fixing of educational aims, arrangement of curricula, inspection of textbooks and regulation of all educational associations. The failure of the Ministry to achieve a uniform, centralized educational system was due primarily to the political disruption that set in after 1916. The Ministry of Education and the educational system itself reflected the unrest within the country. There have been no fewer than ten Ministers of Education in the nineteen years since the Republic was established. The educational system has been reorganized three times in the same period, the curricula changed repeatedly and textbooks completely rewritten at least thrice to meet the varying demands of the political factions that have seized power.

The primary cause of this attempt to maintain an autocratic form of educational system, even under a nominal republic, was the prevailing conception of education as the supreme prerogative of the nation, to be used by it as a tool for promoting national unification. This conception of the value of modern education, which we have already seen was the prevalent one at the close of the Imperial régime, has continued unaltered throughout the period since the establishment of the Republic. During these years of educational confusion and experimentation, two aims have remained consistently clear and repeatedly expressed, namely the need for awakening the people to a self-conscious awareness of their duty to the nation, because of the precarious position which it held in the world, and its logical concomitant—the aim to use the educational system as the means of militarization. Indeed these aims have been pursued with increasing intensity especially since 1925 when the educational system became widely permeated with the philosophy and sentiments of modern nationalism.

The only exception to this general observation, an exception which serves to clarify the rule, occurred in the period from 1919 to 1925 when, due in main, to the extreme disorganization of political life and the attendant decentralization of power, professional educators were able to organize in associations and proceed to build a system of education more in harmony with their professional ideals. They edited texts, planned curricula, improved teaching methods, especially in the field of science, started experimental schools, and, in short, did all that would enable education to meet the real problems of the Chinese. Logically enough it was the period when they moved away from the autocratic educational system of Germany and Japan and imitated in part the decentralized and more democratic American system. But the nationalistic movements which began about 1925 brought that fruitful period to an abrupt close.

One of the first tasks that confronted the newly reorganized Ministry of Education was to re-define educational aims so as to bring them into harmony with the spirit and ideals of a Republic. Then, too, it had to bring about the elimination, from textbooks, of references and material implying the continued existence of the dynasty. Moreover, an attempt was made to reorganize the educational system. Minister Ts'ai was then, as now, more in favor of the French educational system and attempted to get away from the Japanese system at that time, but he was unable to do so.[2] Great importance was laid by the new ministry on social education, the diffusion of knowledge through quasi-educational institutions such as lectures, newspapers, public libraries, etc. to the people as a whole. The necessity of educating the masses to fulfill their duties and functions as citizens of the new Republic lay behind this resort to adult education. A beginning in this form of education was made during the dynasty. Since 1911 it has been more fully developed under the supervision of a special organization in the Ministry. Series of lectures, dramas, etc., have been published for the use of

the local lecture bureaus and many public libraries opened.
Among the topics used in lectures were, " . . . the duties
and privileges of republican citizenship; the importance of
developing a military spirit; the importance of promoting
the economic and industrial welfare of the country; and especially the importance of emphasizing public virtue."[3] The
widespread network of lecture bureaus established after 1912
gave to nationalists' groups an opportunity to disseminate
their propaganda quickly and effectively. Especially was this
revealed to be true at the time of the national student movement of 1919. More recently, since the success of the Mass
Education Movement, as worked out by James Yen and his
associates, has been evident to all, the Ministry has tended
to adopt its technique and conduct its own movement to remove illiteracy.

With this general survey as background, a more detailed
account of the changes made in the educational system, as
the consequence of the establishment of a Republic, will now
be considered. In an order to all educational authorities the
Ministry of Education on May 11, 1912 listed the nine important changes to be made in the educational system at that
time. It requested that the word for school be changed from
"T'ang" to "Hsiao"; that all textbooks be revised so as
to be in harmony with the spirit of a Republican Government; that the Chinese classics be no longer taught in normal,
middle and primary schools; that handiwork courses be emphasized in primary schools; that the use of the abacus be
taught in third year primary arithmetic courses; that boys
and girls study together in lower primary schools; that middle schools, being part of common school education, need
not have departments as in colleges, and that the old literary

degrees be abolished and the students be simply designated as graduates of normal, middle or primary schools.[4]

In order to win the support and have the advice of the leading educators of the country at this critical period of readjustment, the Minister called an Emergency Central Educational Conference which was held in Peking from July 10th to August 19th, 1912. It discussed and made plans for the unification of school regulations; the relation of the Ministry to the provincial and local educational bureaus; the development of education among Tibetans, Mongolians and Mohammedans; the worship of Confucius; the adoption of a national song and the organization of a higher educational conference.[5] The conference submitted to the Ministry some twenty-three resolutions as a possible basis for future action. Though it had no legislative power, these recommendations had a strong influence on the Ministry.[6]

In the September following the close of the conference, Minister Ts'ai issued an order determining the educational aims. These aims were somewhat at variance with those put forth in 1906. He held education to be " . . . a means of cultivating virtuous or moral character in the young. This moral training was to be supplemented by an industrial and military education and rounded out by an aesthetic one."[7] Furthermore, he stated that under the Ch'ing dynasty all educators aimed at a militaristic nation and now Republican China should continue that aim by educating every citizen to be a soldier. His conception of citizenship morality consisted of instilling into the minds of the youths the principles of Liberty, Equality and Fraternity. An analysis of the curricula is given to show the extent to which these four aims were embodied in it. He pointed out that the only real change made in the educational aims with the establishment of the Republic was that education should no longer promote respect for the Emperor; nor should it make Confucianism a state religion as that would be against the principle of religious liberty provided for in the new Constitution. There was, moreover, to be no emphasis on the classics in the lower schools.[8] Ts'ai also revealed another aim of a more definite and concrete nature in a speech before the Senate when he stated that now the "five races" (Chinese, Manchus, Mongolians, Tibetans and Mohammedans) were equal, it meant that all should be equally educated. He informed the Senators that it was especially important to devise plans for the education of the Mongolians, Tibetans, and Mohammedans in the Chinese language and literature as this would serve to unify the Republic.[9] A further evidence of the aim and spirit of education may be seen in an instructional order sent by Minister Ts'ai in the same month to all educational authorities pointing out to them the necessity of educating all women and girls as well as boys and men that China might be as strong as other nations.[10]

President Yüan Shih-k'ai issued many official decrees urging the people to follow Confucius as the one way to strengthen and steady the nation. This was in harmony with his attempt in 1916 to establish a monarchy based on Confucianism. In September, 1913, an order was issued through the Ministry that Confucius' birthday should be observed in the schools by a holiday and the holding of a meeting. This would purify the mind and steady the foundations of the nation.[11] The official worship of Confucius was also restored, and in this connection Yüan Shih-k'ai gave liberally for the rehabilitation of the Hall of Classics and the Confucian temple. Yüan's overthrow and death in 1916 brought an abrupt end to this attempted revival of Confucianism.[12]

However conservative Yüan may appear in the eyes of modern Chinese in his attempted revival of Confucianism as well as in his monarchical ambitions, he was quite modern in his ideas as to patriotism and the duty of the individual to the state. In an address on the occasion of the anniversary of the establishment of the Republic, October 10, 1914, he addressed the students of China presenting to them three principles of patriotism. The first was that all the members of the nation should be upright in their public activities. Secondly, each should strive to become economically self-sustaining as that was the only way in which the nation could become independent. Finally, it was necessary to promote the spirit of militarism and to develop strong bodies. The nation could become strong, he concluded, only through the active practise of these three principles.[13]

In order to continue the survey of developing educational aims and policies as influenced by the rising nationalist spirit under the Republic a summary of the important resolutions and motions adopted at the outstanding educational conferences from 1915 to 1928 will be given. While the chronological presentation adopted entails some repetition, it best serves to reveal the crescendo of demand for a nationalistic type of education and the close relation between the presentation of these demands and the treatment accorded China by the other nations. The first National Conference of Provincial Educational Associations was held at Tientsin during April, 1915. There were twenty-nine representatives from eighteen provinces; two from the Ministry of Education and one from the Ministry of War. The latter representative was quite effective apparently, for among the thirteen resolutions passed one concerned itself with a plan for the militarization of the country. In closing the meeting the Minister of Education T'ang Hua-lung made an address stating that hereafter two points should be especially emphasized by educators. The first was that among the youth industrious habits and the spirit of independence should be cultivated, and the other was that they should be taught to be patriotic and public-spirited. Only in that way could the "national shame" be obliterated and the foundations of the nation be made firm.[14]

From 1916 on, we note a new spirit among educators. They commenced to grasp their problems more realistically and to adopt toward them a more professional spirit. In the first place, industrial education was assiduously promoted. Apparently much criticism was rife, among the public at large, of the industrial schools as they then existed, so educators turned to the task of coördinating these schools with industrial organizations in order that graduates might be fitted to enter industrial life upon graduation.[15] For that purpose an industrial education conference was held in October, 1917.

Numerous other national conferences were held in this period from 1915-1922. The Ministry of Education was relying more and more on them to promote education. Educators became primarily concerned with the immediate problems of education itself. They commenced to organize themselves into associations. We find the Ministry of Education, in February, 1917, issuing a decree ordering all students, teachers, and officers not to enlist in political parties or engage in political activities.[16] An attempt was being made to free the educational system of ulterior political influences.

A spirit of dissatisfaction with the educational system arose, resulting in April 1919, in the first Conference for the Investigation of Education. Sixty of the outstanding educational leaders including Ts'ai Yüan-p'ei, Chiang Monlin, Ch'ên Pao-Ch'üan, and Fan Yüan-lien were appointed to carry out the investigation. This Conference discussed among other things the question of educational aims. The old educational aim, promulgated in September, 1912, was abandoned because of its emphasis on military education. The wave of idealism which marked the close of the World War reached to the Far East and these educators felt and expressed the opinion that the educational aim of China should change in order to be in harmony with that of world opinion, which was for a period actively opposed to militarism of the German variety. However, it was necessary to continue physical education. The new aim adopted sought the cultivation of a strong and developed personality, and the development of the spirit of republicanism. These educators felt that the political chaos obtaining at that time in China was due to a lack of a republican spirit, which they defined as being a sense of responsibility on the part of the Chinese toward the nation itself. They pointed out the differences in educational aims and ideals of Germany, England, France and the United States and made the suggestion that the aim and spirit of American education should henceforth be followed.[17] The fifth annual meeting of the National Federation of Educational Associations endorsed this change of aim.[18]

It has already been noted that China's first modern educational system of 1903 was modelled after that of Japan.[19] The Japanese system was of course in turn modelled for the most part upon that of Germany. With the establishment of the Republic there were a few administrative changes, but the 1903 system continued for the most part.[20] Republican educators such as Ts'ai Yüan-p'ei were aware of the inconsistency of continuing such a type of education, but, as we have seen, were unable to change it. As a matter of fact in the course of the World War when the educators were moved to an actual further revision of the educational system they found after investigation "... the German system best."[21] However, with the defeat of Germany, the prestige of the German educational system rapidly vanished and with it all attempts to imitate it. The popularity of the Japanese system also declined following the presentation of the Twenty-one Demands in the spring of 1915. This paved the way for the introduction of the American school system after 1920, forecast in the statement above.

The conditions enabling the development of a strong and perfected personality, as conceived by the above mentioned conference of outstanding educators, were in the first place the existence of two spheres of moral conduct, the one relating to the individual in order that he might survive, and the other to the public so as to form the basis of his relationship to society and the nation. Secondly, the individual must have the knowledge and the ability to meet the demands and needs of daily life; he must have a strong and active body and a buoyant and happy disposition. The republican spirit was defined as that spirit which develops the democratic concept and brings to the consciousness of the people the knowledge that they form the foundation of the nation. It also develops among the people a power of self-control with respect to public affairs and a corresponding sense of responsibility toward society or the nation.[22] These aims were dominant from that time until about 1925.

For another reflection of the spirit prevailing among educators at the close of the World War we turn to a consideration of the resolutions of the fourth annual conference of the National Federation of Educational Associations held in 1918. One of the motions passed dealt with the special phases to be emphasized in the educational programs in view of that war. The educators were more deeply impressed than ever with the necessity of strengthening the nation. They suggested, therefore, that more mining and industrial schools be opened, that the Boy Scout movement be advocated in order to develop independence and initiative among the boys; that the teaching of science be promoted together with physical and industrial education, and above all that the principles and practises of citizenship be taught in order to establish a democratic form of government in which the citizen would be the foundation of the nation.[23] The conception of citizenship as held by the Americans and the French commenced to take form in the minds of the educators at this time (though the idea was propagated and discussed from the establishment of the Republic) and was to reach the zenith of its influence, as will be noted in more detail below, in the years between 1922-1925.

This same conference also urged the establishment of clubs for young men, as all nations have such organizations and use them as a means for controlling the youth. The purpose was to cultivate patriotism and citizenship. These clubs were to include not only students, but others from the community not in school. Any prominent members of the community were to be officers and the money was to be secured from any group. These clubs were to be a factor in guiding educational matters in the community.[24] This was indeed a veritable *carte blanche* giving any so-called "student club" or "young men's club" the right to run the local school system. It was both a recognition of a condition and a stimulus to its development. In the attitude thus revealed on the part of responsible educators toward the young men we find a cause for the mushroom-like growth of all sorts of "student clubs" which have been the cause of so much disruption and lack of discipline in school life and have engaged the students in all sorts of political movements at the expense of their formal education. This attitude sprang chiefly from two causes; the first and more fundamental one being the survival of the old prerogatives and privileges of the literati as a class and their superior position in the nation to all other groups; and secondly the generally low grade of ability and personality to be found among the majority of teachers at this time. The students, having little respect for them and keenly aware of their own importance, played a rôle in school and national affairs out of all proportion to their numbers and ability.

This conference also placed special emphasis on the promotion of physical education. It was observed that the World War had clearly revealed the necessity for physico-military education if a nation was to exist in a world of warring states. It was for that reason that all countries, and especially Japan, promoted it. It was suggested that men be sent abroad to study physical education and that courses in it be required in the normal schools. Each province and city should organize physical-education associations. And in the same resolution it was urged that military training in the schools be extended, that fighting technique be developed by special forms of physical drill such as fencing, boxing, etc. This was to be promoted through lectures, athletic meets and exhibitions.[25] The Ministry of Education endorsed this plan for physical education and ordered it to be carried out.[26]

The marked emphasis on physical education at this time and its close relationship to military education is further seen in the action taken at the National Conference of Middle School Principals held in 1918. At that conference a resolution was passed advocating the adoption of military training in all middle schools in order to develop the physique of the youth, also in order to provide for the future protection of the country. The resolution requested that each higher normal school and physical education department establish special military training departments or sub-departments.[27]

The Boy Scout movement, which significantly enough arose in the spirit of these times, was not then, nor has it since, been divorced from a military connotation. It was viewed as a means for arousing students to an interest in physical and military education. It was to be a sort of preliminary training to be conducted among primary school students principally to prepare them (mentally, no doubt) for the time when they had attained a physical development that would enable them later to carry on full-fledged military drill. The use of the character *chün* or "army" in the Chinese term for Boy Scout is a token of its militaristic flavour. By February, 1919, the movement had grown to such an extent that the Ministry of Education, with a view to controlling it, asked that information concerning the various organizations be sent in. The object of the movement as stated by the Ministry at that time was to cultivate in the youth the sentiment of public and national loyalty as well as the habit of obeying regulations.[28]

At the fifth annual conference of the National Federation of Educational Associations held late in the year 1919 a resolution was passed to expand the Boy Scout movement. All normal schools were to add courses without delay. Regulations as to the mode of organization, activities and uniforms were to be the same throughout the nation. Books on the movement in other countries were to be translated. Every year there was to be a national gathering of Scouts.[29]

The above conference defined anew the educational aims and methods. Professor John Dewey was in China at the time and his influence and that of other progressive American educators became important for the next few years, considerably modifying the educational system. Chinese educators such as P. W. Kuo, Chiang Monlin, Hu Shih, and others trained in the United States, were beginning to make their influence felt. Professor John Dewey was followed by Professors Paul Monroe, G. R. Twiss, and William A. McCall who were influential in bringing about a reorganization along American lines of the school system including teaching methods, the curricula, and textbooks. The aims adopted at this conference will indicate the beginning of this period of growth and reorganization. The conference felt that hereafter the educators of the land should work more in harmony with one another and not look solely to the Ministry of Education for guidance relying more on their own initiative. It was felt that the curricula were overcrowded. The need was expressed for more scientific apparatus that the students might conduct their own experiments. It was suggested that libraries be expanded. It was felt that students should "learn by doing." Model school cities or school republics were to be organized in order to develop the concepts of citizenship and the attendant virtues of responsible self-control. The students were to be encouraged to serve society (the term coming now to mean society in general and not the more narrow conception of the nation as such) and the relation between school and society was to be very intimate. Everything was to be done to let the students develop their own individual aptitudes.[30]

At the sixth annual conference of the National Federation of Educational Associations held in the fall of 1920 there were several resolutions passed that were of especial interest as indicating educational thought-trends during this period. One of these concerned itself with the promotion of Chinese education among Mongols and Tibetans, that they might be moulded into a civilization similar to that of China (*t'ung hua*). This was held to be one of the chief duties of the educational system, as only in that way could the five races of the Republic become united and equal.[31] Another resolution planned for the democratization of educational control whereby teachers, students, local administrators, and the people of the community might have a larger share in the conduct of educational affairs than had been the case in the past. This was quite in harmony with the political and administrative tendencies of the period. Federalism was the popular word in political circles and a Federal Constitution had been actually drawn up.[32]

This conference also passed a resolution for the promotion of student self-government. It said in part, now that China was a Republic, the people had a right to rule, and in order to rule, they should be animated by a love of the nation.

If the people participate in the government of the nation they will develop a sense of responsibility. As the students would be the future leaders of the land it was asserted that they should be given a chance to develop this sense of responsibility through student self-government. The aim of these student self-governing organizations was to develop among the students a sense of responsible citizenship.[38]

At this juncture occurred the Student Movement of 1919 which grew directly out of the award to Japan by the Paris Peace Conference of the German leaseholds in Shantung. It will be necessary to appraise the influence of this movement on the developing educational system. This effect was practically negligible save that, as Hu Shih admits, it served to hasten the official adoption of the *pai hua,* or vernacular language in primary schools. The immediate result of the movement was to make the students more politically minded, to create among them greater lack of discipline than before and to cause an increase in the number of school strikes. Responsible educators since that time have voiced again and again the necessity of getting the students to return to the school and to forsake political activities. In the national sphere the movement, which was the culmination of a whole series of lesser ones of the same nature that preceded and which continued to grow, was basically a nationalist movement on the part of the most nationalistic element in Chinese society. In 1919 the students for the first time carried to some degree their spirit to the laboring and farming classes, whereas before it had scarcely extended beyond commercial circles. Through public lectures and all the approved methods of modern propagandists they carried not only the nationalistic message, but added to it the message of social and individual, economic and educational salvation to millions of the poor and the illiterate. As a result of the movement the students have had a greater degree of concern for the worker and the peasant. It was to lead them in later years to embrace socialism and communism. Nevertheless, whether the students later became socialists or communists, they were primarily nationalists. Social and economic reform they stated should be guided by the national state, equal and sovereign among the other states of the world.[34]

The third annual meeting of the Society for the Advancement of Education was held at Nanking in July, 1924 with about two thousand in attendance. Among the matters stressed were education by foreign missionaries, and education among Chinese emigrants and the Mongolians. The aim of education among the Mongolians as set forth in a resolution was to treat them equally and not to discriminate against them racially. A Mongolian Educational Committee was to be established for the purpose of drawing up suitable textbooks, of collecting Mongolian literature and of promoting lectures on Mongolian life and customs. The government was requested to provide for the establishment and financing of a Mongolian University.[35] Throughout this period, as we have had occasion to note, there was a lively interest among the educators at their annual conferences in the promotion of Chinese education among the Tibetans as well as the Mongolians. The aim, as always, was to bring the culture of these people more into harmony with that of China in order to consolidate the Republic. Care was taken, however, not to appear racially or culturally superior. Though these peoples were to be taught Chinese literature and language, yet Mongolian and Tibetan literature and language were to be cherished and taught as well. It was to be a bilingual, bi-cultural education. Lack of finance and political disorder have prevented to the present the carrying out of these plans to any great degree.

The third annual conference of the Association for the Advancement of Education, in 1924, passed some resolutions of special interest. One motion provided for the establishment of a Japanese Research Society. The purpose was to study the methods whereby Japan made itself strong and independent. The resolution stated that Sino-Japanese relations should be especially emphasized. In connection with this resolution it was decided that on the National Humiliation Day, when the Twenty-one Demands were accepted, especial effort should be put forth to arouse the people to the need for coöperation against Japan. This could be done by setting forth in detail the humiliating history of the relations between the two countries. A comparison of the development of the two countries should also be presented and the sources of China's weakness and Japan's strength emphasized. Leaders in each locality were to devise ways and means for carrying out this program on National Humiliation days.[36] At the same time that the conference was held there was an educational exhibit the aims of which were among others to promote "love for the fatherland," citizenship, foreign commerce and, finally, the education of Chinese overseas.[37]

The killing of Chinese students and civilians at Shanghai in May, 1925, and at Canton in June, as well as at a number of other points, by foreign forces led to intense and wide spread reaction. The spirit of nationalism grew and intensified to a point unattained before. The effect on the educational system was immediate. At the eleventh conference of the Federated Provincial Educational Associations, held in Changsha in October of that year, the educational aims were defined anew. At this conference there were present thirty-eight representatives from eighteen provinces and five special areas. This group decided that henceforth education should emphasize the racial peculiarities of China. All the history and civics textbooks were to contain material designed to arouse the racial consciousness of the students. Those in charge of social education were to spread the same idea through lectures, novels, and the drama. The primary texts were to adopt pictures inspiring a feeling of shame at the indignities suffered by the nation at the hands of foreigners. Stories were to be given to arouse their patriotism. Also the schools were to emphasize military training.[38] Once again we note the immediate effect of the treatment accorded the nation in the international sphere reflected upon the educational aims and the textbooks. The educational system has been revealed as the most sensitive register of influences arising out of international relations. The growth of militarism, and the more objectionable forms of strident nationalism were a direct outgrowth of the nation's unfortunate treatment at the hands of the rest of the world.

The effect of this intensified nationalist movement upon the educational system will now be traced. The Association for the Advancement of Education, which, from the time it was organized in 1921, had been liberal in its educational policy, submitted to the nationalistic viewpoint after May, 1925. A survey of the resolutions and addresses made at its fourth annual conference held in Tai-yuan clearly revealed this. Over one thousand delegates assembled at that place including ten delegates from Mongolia and twenty-seven from Tibet. The opening address was delivered by T'ao Chih-hsing, an ardent nationalist, who stated that education must aim primarily to develop patriotism as a result of the May 30th (1925) affair in Shanghai when foreign forces shot and killed Chinese. As the conference was held in the northwest for the convenience of Mongolian and Tibetan educators he appealed to them to promote, along with the Chinese, the spirit of Republicanism and equality among the five races.[39]

The need for a further nationalization of the educational system at this time was felt to be so great that a motion was passed asking the Ministry of Education to change the educational aims so as to be in harmony with that ideal. In outline the motion urged that education should place emphasis on the culture of China in order to spread a knowledge of the nation's characteristics among the students. Then too, military education should be further promoted. More emphasis was to be placed upon the humiliating experiences which the nation had passed through, in order to call forth patriotic sentiment. And finally scientific education was to be advanced that the roots of knowledge and talent might flourish. A motion was passed to fix the educational prerogatives and aims in the Constitution of the Republic. Another motion advocated the establishment of military training in the middle and higher schools. The purpose was to develop a militaristic people.[40] Another motion stated that girls, as well as boys, should be disciplined in military tactics that their bodies might be strengthened. Military exercises were held very good for this and as the girls would become the mothers of the nation they needed strong bodies. In Girls'

Normal Schools, therefore, courses in military drill and physical training were to be given.[41]

Other motions passed in harmony with this nationalistic spirit provided that in primary schools the textbooks should emphasize materials relating to the humilating episodes in China's international relations. Readers, histories, and geographies should all contain these materials. Another motion endorsed the action of the National Federation of Educational Associations at its tenth annual conference in 1924 that courses in the English language be removed from primary schools and be made elective only in junior middle schools.[42] The conference devoted two special sections to Mongolian and Tibetan education. Plans for extending the Chinese educational system to these areas were made. However, the native literatures and languages were to be retained.[43]

The nationalization of the educational system has continued apace from May, 1925 to the present. The greatest impetus to the development came with the nominal unification of the country under the Kuomintang after May, 1928, with the capital at Nanking. This party is avowedly nationalistic and the greater portion of its program and policies are framed from that viewpoint and carried out in that spirit. Favouring a centralized bureaucratic government it was natural that in its educational policy it should strive for the same aims. Ts'ai Yüan-p'ei became the President of the University Council, a new organization set up temporarily to replace the Ministry of Education. In May, 1928 he convened the first national educational conference under the new nationalist régime. The meeting took place in Nanking and was attended by seventy-seven delegates representing the whole nation. It is interesting to note that, of these seventy-seven men, forty-nine had studied abroad: twenty-eight in the United States, eleven in Japan, and ten in Europe.

The educational aims as redefined by this conference brought education into harmony with the Kuomintang ideology epitomized in the "Three Principles of the People" as presented by the party's leader, Dr. Sun Yat-sen. This was to be known as "San Min Chu I education." With this type of education the nation was to be firmly established upon a developed Republican form of government. San Min Chu I education meant not only that Sun's teachings were to be embodied in the textbooks, but that educators were to seek to promote in reality the spirit of racialism and cultural self-consciousness in order to put into practice the three principles of the people: Nationalism (Racialism), Democracy, and Livelihood. Educators should cultivate obedience to, and observance of, the law; discipline the students in the spirit of coöperation and in the spirit and technique of Republican government, that the people's rights may in reality become established. They should promote the labor movement, scientific education, and the arts, that the idea and the reality of the people's livelihood might flourish.[44] Other concrete programs advocated by those educational leaders were plans for securing independence of educational finance; a request that the Central Political Council look into the matter of controlling the student movements; plans for the encouragement and promotion of Chinese education among overseas Chinese; and schemes whereby to promote the use of national goods, as, for example, by advocating the passing of laws compelling the purchase of scientific apparatus made in China.[45]

The conference was divided into sections one of which was devoted to physical and military education. Through this section a motion was adopted to provide for student army officers' training corps in senior middle schools and higher schools. It was resolved that army officers should be provided to conduct military drill in the schools. During the school year three hours a week of this drill were to be required. Then every summer for three weeks the boys were to be put through an intensive drill. The object was to teach the students the care of the body, obedience, the sense of responsibility and a willingness to do physical work and, above all, to arouse in them a spirit of service to the nation. In the junior middle schools both Boy and Girl Scout organizations were to be promoted. For the girls in senior middle schools and higher schools, nurses' training was to be provided. It was the belief of the conference that the development of physico-military education was the most important way in which to save the country and should, therefore, receive the earnest attention of educators. It was stated that since the World War all nations emphasized this type of education. One of the speeches eloquently urged China to follow the methods of Imperial Germany in educating the youth in the spirit and practise of militarism.[46]

That there should be a complete revision of the textbooks on the advent to power of this revolutionary party was a foregone conclusion. In the conference a motion was passed that all teaching materials in the primary and middle schools should be selected so as to emphasize the humiliating experiences through which the nation had passed in its international relations during the last century in order to arouse among the students a deep racial consciousness.[47]

Other evidence of the nationalistic spirit among the educators in office at this time may be seen in a motion "to blend" the five races and develop and expand their civilization. This could only mean one thing, and that to spread Chinese ideals among the Manchus, Mohammedans, Mongolians, and Tibetans. However, it was stipulated that the local languages and literature were to be respected. A motion was also adopted to promote education among the border tribes.[48] Another motion provided for the use of the national language (Kuo Yü) in the schools in order to unify the racial spirit and firmly establish the foundations of the nation.[49] In connection with this was a motion ordering all the readers in primary schools to be written in the Mandarin vernacular (Pai Hua). Also in connection with this a motion was passed opposing the use of foreign languages in the primary schools. Moreover entrance requirements to middle schools were not to be in any foreign language.[50] This was a reaction chiefly to missionary education with its emphasis on English instruction.

Continuing the interest of educators, noted above, in nationalizing emigrants, the conference passed a motion advocating the development of Chinese education among the ten million overseas Chinese. The avowed purpose was to preserve international peace by maintaining in the sphere of international relations liberty and equality, also in order to enable China to establish itself as a nation and to preserve the Chinese racial integrity wherever individual Chinese might choose to reside.[51] This movement to educate overseas Chinese was imperialistic, for it attempted in places, especially in the Nan Yang (South Seas) area, to "re-Sinicize"

Chinese who had been resident many generations abroad and had become citizens of other countries. The conference agreed that some of the returned Boxer indemnity money might be used for the purpose of educating, in China, Chinese whose homes were abroad.[52]

In the days before they had succeeded in nominally unifying the nation at Nanking, the Kuomintang members had called their type of education *Tang Hua,* or "Party Transformation Education." It was decided at this conference that such a name gave rise to undue suspicions among the people at large and hence it was decided to change the name to *"San Min Chu I* education."[53] This would identify education in the public mind, with the philosophy and teachings of Dr. Sun, and not with the peculiar interpretations and methods adopted by the party to carry out his broad and rather vague principles.

With this conference is concluded the survey of the influence of modern nationalism on the developing educational aims and policies as revealed in the principal educational conferences since the establishment of the Republic. The following chapter traces more in detail the effect of these aims upon the curricula and on the content of the textbooks used in the schools.

CHAPTER IV

NATIONALISM AND CHINESE TEXTBOOKS

The textbooks used in the modern schools of China follow closely the changing educational aims and curricula outlined in the preceding chapters. Therefore, there were frequent revisions and more often complete changes in the texts themselves as the digest of those more extensively used (Appendix I) reveals. This is due to the extension of the same autocratic, centralized control that obtained in theory and for the most part in practice with regard to all other phases of the educational system. From its inception the Ministry of Education maintained the policy of passing upon all textbooks published by private houses and giving its approval to those which should be used in the schools. The officers and teachers were repeatedly ordered to use only those texts obtaining its approval. Though this policy frequently worked to eliminate texts that were pedagogically unsound and scientifically inaccurate and thus resulted in higher standards, the dominant aim was to unify the educational system, that all the people might be educated to the same viewpoint, that all might become patriotic and effective members or citizens of the state, that it might in turn be strengthened to maintain its proper place of independence and equality in a world of warring states.

In the first part of 1906 the newly established Ministry

of Education set up a special bureau to survey texts and issued twenty-two regulations to govern its activities. The order in part is as follows:

This (Ministry) is put in charge of the education of the whole Empire. Now that our country is at the inception of its educational system it is important that we secure unity of administration and see that the principles on which action is based are correct. We therefore give first attention to schoolbooks. Pending the time when the Board (Ministry) will issue its own books we shall select the books printed by the various publishers and approve those that are suitable in order to provide for the needs of the schools.[1]

Noteworthy here is the implication that the Ministry went so far as to plan to publish the texts itself. This plan was soon abandoned as it proved to be beyond the resources of the Ministry. Mr. Wong Yun-wu, the editor-in-chief of the Commercial Press, which publishes about 60 per cent of the textbooks, told the writer in a personal interview, that the Ministry of Education at Nanking had, in 1928, expressed a similar desire to publish the texts, but had likewise found it impossible to do so.

In the summer of 1912, following the establishment of the Republic, the new Ministry of Education devised a plan for establishing provincial investigating committees.[2] This plan was abolished in January, 1914 when the Ministry assumed the whole task and at the same time issued minute regulations concerning the publication and examination of books. The Ministry, on the basis of these regulations, proceeded to deal directly with the publishing houses.[3] Such has been the arrangement with slight modifications from that time to the present. Of course the vigor with which the inspection was conducted varied greatly. The censorship was never more vigorously carried out than under the present Ministry, instituted by the Nationalist government at Nanking, since early 1928. This was the expressed opinion of the heads of the two largest publishing houses, the Commerical Press and the Chung Hua Press, to the author in the spring of 1929. The publishers on their part of course found it profitable to meet the demands of the educators whose support would, of course, greatly increase the sales of approved books.

Curricula and textbooks were compiled in close harmony with the aims adopted in 1912. In the Appendix will be found a survey of a number of textbooks of this time which will reveal how the spirit back of these aims was instilled into the minds of the youth.[4] The aims to be achieved in primary schools were set forth by the Ministry in November, 1912. The minds of the students were to be formed so as to lead to virtuous conduct. They were instructed to be filial, fraternal and altruistic, to be morally courageous, to respect themselves and others; to be zealous in their work and to be economical. They were to have practical instruction in all things necessary for the common existence. Above all, they were to be instructed in social and civic virtues that they might follow the way of progress and work for the good of the fatherland. This was set forth in the first article.[5] The second article amplified this aim by setting forth the object of the course on ethics or self-culture *(hsiu shên)*.

The object of the course on moral instruction is to develop the virtue of the children that they might do good. The virtues which lower primary school students should have are obedience, love, faith, braveness, respect, politeness, diligence and a pure mind. Those virtues easier to teach should be first selected and later those virtues relating to the community and finally to the nation should be taught. The spirit of patriotism should be instilled that the children might come to love their countrymen and the nation.[6]

The higher primary schools were to amplify and perfect these same aims.

In the lower primary school the only history and geography taught was to be found in the little readers and in the ethical texts. Practically nothing of the outside world was given.[7] The object of teaching history in the higher primary schools was to let the children know the general condition of the whole nation in order to inspire them to be good nationals (*kuo-min*). The history of China was to begin with Huang Ti (the mythological emperor reputed to have founded the Empire) and to be followed by an outline of the chief events of the various dynasties together with the deeds and words of the great men. The origin of Eastern Asiatic civilization was to be given; also an account of the establishment of the Republic and the relation of China to the other nations during the past century. This course was to be closely associated with the one on ethics.[8] The course on geography was to impart a knowledge of the world at large, of the conditions that make for human existence, especially of the Chinese for the purpose of developing among the children the spirit of nationalism and the love of the fatherland. An analysis of the conditions within China and its political and economic relations with the other nations was the primary purpose of the courses in geography, though a general survey of the more important countries was to be given. The children were also to be taught the geography of their native district that they might have a love for the place of their birth as well as for the nation as a whole.[9] After treating in this manner of the substance and object of the other courses taught in the primary schools the regulation concluded by stating that in teaching these courses the teacher should always show to the students the peculiar characteristics of "our country" that a patriotic consciousness might be evoked.[10] The only instruction on the history and geography of the world at large was relegated to the last half of the last year of higher primary schools.[11]

In middle schools, the course on ethical culture was taught one hour a week for the four years. In the first year the aim was to teach the general relation of man to his world; in the second, children were to be taught their duty toward the nation as the supreme social grouping; in the third, their duty to their race and to themselves. Finally, in the fourth year, the general principles of ethics were to be set forth together with the peculiar characteristics and virtues of China. In history the first and second years were to be devoted entirely to Chinese history. In the third and fourth years the history of eastern Asia and of the West was to be taught. In geography the greater part of the first two years was devoted to that of China alone; the third year dealt with foreign countries, while the fourth year gave a general outline of natural and human geography. Physical education was to be given three hours a week, and military drill was required.[12]

The Ministry of Education further amplified its wishes at this time concerning the nature and value of the course on geography and history. It was held to be a means of presenting to the youth the status of China in the world not only from a geographical, but also from a political point of view. The weakness of China under the ruthless pressure of the western nations was to be revealed. This was to arouse in the students a sense of shame and of patriotism and urge them to strive to build an independently strong country. The strategic aspects of China's boundaries and communications and their significance from a naval and military point of view were also to be stressed. In short the course on geography was to be looked upon as one of the chief means for arousing in the future responsible members of the new Republic a sense of national patriotism and the desire to work for the salvation of the nation.[13] In the teaching of history China's former high position in Eastern Asia was to be contrasted with its present weakness as a means for arousing the students to aid the nation. The difference between a monarchy and a republic was to be emphasized in order to arouse the students' loyalty to the new régime.[14]

Three outstanding conclusions may be derived from the above outline of curricula content and aims as worked out in the first two years of the Republic. The first is that over 95 per cent of those educated in China under this system received no knowledge of the world outside of China. Furthermore, the additional 2 per cent, or more, in middle schools, received such information so distorted by being passed through the lens of the national perspective that it had practically no value in creating in the citizen a consciousness of the World Community. The second is the elimination from both primary and middle schools of the formal teaching of the classics. The third is that Chinese educators had grasped the fact that an awareness of the nation's cultural heritage, of its place in the world, of its peculiar characteristics can be instilled into the students through all the courses, especially those on geography, history, and ethics. The realization of this fact enabled educators to drop the classics without fear of failing to attain the supreme aim of the educational system.

The Normal school curricula were of course a reflection of those of the middle and primary schools. For example in the course on ethics, which was taught one hour a week the aim was to instruct the teachers in their duty to the country, to society, the family, and the race. The last year of the course emphasized the peculiar characteristics of the Chinese nation. Military drill along with physical exercise was required four hours a week of the prospective teachers.[15]

In the period from 1913-1916 there was a strong tendency to restore the classics to their former place of importance in the curricula. This was due to the monarchical leanings of Yüan Shih-k'ai. In May, 1914 the Minister of Education Tang Hua-lung, who had succeeded Ts'ai Yüan-p'ei, issued a general statement to the writers of textbooks that the ethical readers should place more emphasis on the teachings of Confucius. The aim was to make Confucianism the national religion. He pointed out that even under the monarchy there was a tendency to drop the classics as the content was too obscure and mature for the children and the curricula too crowded with other courses. In the summer before the Revolution at the first Central Educational Conference it was decided to offer certain classical instruction in the courses on ethics and let the classics as a whole be dropped. Thus the educators aimed to preserve only in outline the teachings of Confucius and that was what the Ministry of Education wished to revive at that time.[16]

The following month the Minister sent an order to all primary and middle schools stating that more classical instruction should be incorporated in the course on ethical culture. President Yüan had especially ordered this to be done. The Minister pointed out that in the West the Bible was a regular course, while in Japan the doctrine of the heavenly origin of the Imperial family and its continuous existence through countless generations was preached. China should, therefore, found itself on Confucian morality. All book publishers were cautioned to observe this order. It was contended that if the order was carried out the morality of the people would be improved and the nation made strong.[17]

In spite of the attempted centralized control of the publication of schoolbooks we find many published and used in the schools which did not obtain the approval of the Ministry. This conclusion may be drawn from a communication addressed to all the provincial bureaus of education, in 1917, ordering all draft copies of texts on ethics and literature to be sent to the Ministry for its inspection and approval. The communication stated that many writers did not do that. During two years (1915-1917), the Ministry asserted, it had been giving especial attention to these two classes of texts as they were of utmost importance in national education. By June of 1918, the Ministry ordered all provincial educational bureaus to report on the texts in use or in process of publication. The communication closed with the significant remark that as the country was greatly disturbed it became very necessary to improve texts and promote education in order to stabilize the nation.[18]

Beginning about this time (1917) there arose an active and widespread discussion and criticism of the textbooks teaching ethical culture. These were held to be the most important texts in molding the thought life and emotional attitudes of the students with respect to the state. As an indication of this interest and also of the intimate influence of one nation's textbooks on another we find an article in the official magazine of the Ministry of Education for February, 1919. The article was translated from Japanese and was entitled, "The Duty of Giving Courses on *Hsiu Shên*" ("Ethical Culture"). It traced the history of this type of course in other lands pointing out that France first adopted it in the 1880's and Italy in the 'nineties. It pointed out that nowhere was religion taught in this course, but that the object was to impress upon the youth their nation's peculiar virtues and destiny.

When Chinese educators commenced to eliminate the classics, the need was felt for some sort of moral instruction. They followed the example of Japan where already these *hsiu shên* texts had been written to supply a similar need. The Japanese in turn had been conscious of how western nations arrived at the same result. In all cases the aim was primarily to instill into the youth patriotic devotion to their own state along with the inculcation of certain elemental individual and social ethics.

It was about this time also that Chinese educators as a group grasped the concept of citizenship (Kung Min). In 1914 there appeared a book by Weng Chang-chung called "The Model Citizen."[19] This book had a wide sale and was no doubt very influential in preparing the way for the civics readers which commenced to be used after 1920. In his preface the author criticized the *hsiu shên,* or ethical readers, as being inadequate for the new day when the citizen's relation to society was the supreme duty. The old loyalty to the family must be extended to include the nation and even the world. Seeing this need in China the author selected passages from famous western writers on the general subject of citizenship, translated them and gave them forth to help his country in the way of moral education. Many of the translations were drawn from the utterances of outstanding western patriots setting forth a nationalistic interpretation of the duties and responsibilities of citizenship.

Owing to these influences a few of the leading educators reached the decision that the *hsiu shên* texts must give way to civics readers modelled after those used in the West. At the fifth conference of the National Educational Association held late in 1919 two resolutions were passed bearing on this change. One of these provided for the general revision of primary and middle school textbooks. Many of the teachers felt that more local material should be put in the texts and less of a nationalistic nature. The conference consented to this, but insisted that the texts emphasize such general material of a national nature as would awaken in the students the conceptions and responsibilities of national citizenship. The other resolution in harmony with this provided for the selection and editing of materials designed to attain this end. The resolution stated that the authority and power of the Republic was invested in its citizens. That right was fixed in the Constitution and in that respect China was in harmony with other states. Therefore the conclusion arrived at was that it became necessary to teach the students the duties and responsibilities of citizenship. According to a revised regulation on *kuo min* education, decreed in October, 1916, one of the chief objects of the *hsiu shên* courses was to teach the children "what a citizen ought to know."[20] As in higher primary and middle schools such courses had not yet been given, it was ordered, therefore, that such texts on citizenship should be published and introduced into the system beginning with the third year of primary schools. For the use of lecturers in the popular educational system a reference book on citizenship was also to be published. The purpose was to enable lecturers to present material of better quality to the people before whom they appeared.[21]

This same conference also outlined what the new civics readers should contain. The text was to be divided into four parts: Hygiene, Morality, Law, and Economics. The resolution stated that citizenship was especially emphasized in the modern world. "Formerly men cherished the family and racial viewpoint, but now men should cherish the social and world viewpoint." This statement clearly reflects the liberalism existing among educators during this period. With regard to health and hygiene the citizens were to be taught how to strengthen their bodies. *Tao-tê,* or the way of virtuous and moral conduct, was considered the foundation of individual character. This could be best taught through presenting the exemplary lives of great men. All types of moral virtue, arising out of social relationships extending from the family, the community, and the race to the national, the industrial, and the international society, were to be taught. In the section on law emphasis was to be placed on the national legal system and its function in unifying and ordering the national society. Potential citizens were to be taught their civil functions and responsibilities. The fundamental principles of international law were to be taught as well. In the economic section national economy was to be stressed that students might become aware of the processes by which the nation gained its livelihood. They were also to be informed on industrial and labor problems. The resolution further included a detailed outline of the contents of the series.²²

In the Citizenship Education section of the fourth annual conference of the Association for the Advancement of Education of 1925, two interesting motions were adopted. One suggested that the middle schools promote Confucian morality as a means of developing the "people's character" in order to remove the causes of disorder and strengthen the foundations of the nation.²³ It was moved by Liu K'un-shu. During the previous year he had been a delegate to the World Conference of Federated Educational Associations where, he informed his colleagues, a motion had been passed to emphasize education for character with a view to stressing the child's place in society. He pointed out that in China this type of education was known as *Tao-tê* education, and that it could best be taught through the classics. Mr. Liu said he wanted this type of education taught in the interests of world peace, and especially to quiet and strengthen China. He thought too much emphasis was being placed on scientific and industrial education which might, or might not, strengthen the character of the people.²⁴

The other motion provided that adult education and citizenship education should emphasize the general principles of Republican government in order to cultivate among all citizens a sense of responsibility.²⁵ In this connection it is interesting to note that in a motion passed providing for teaching the conditions and needs of village and community life in village schools, educators recognized the existence of many kinds of *kung min,* just as formerly they had recognized varying forms of *hsiu shên.* That is to say they believed there was a village, a district, a provincial, and a world citizenship as well as a national citizenship.[26] It is an indication of the practical and analytical tendencies of the highly developed moral philosophy of the Chinese. It is in striking contrast to western moral philosophies in lacking a metaphysical foundation; but springs rather from the actual social groupings of Chinese society and a keen awareness of the individual and social consequences of every act. Nationalism in China, as elsewhere in its cruder extreme forms, has tended to suppress in and even to eliminate from, the school system material dealing with other and more fundamental social groupings both within and without the nation, in its overpowering aim to make students supremely conscious of the state as the single and dominant social grouping.

At the 1923 conference of the Society for the Advancement of Education, a motion was presented by the primary school teachers that more space, at least two-thirds, be devoted to materials dealing with local and community life and problems. There were heated discussions at two of the plenary sessions, and it was only in the fourth session, after a lengthy discussion, that the motion in a modified form was adopted. The opposition pointed out that textbooks in other countries devoted more than one-third the space to material of a national character. The motion, as adopted, said nothing about the relative amount of space to be devoted to the two sorts of material. In substance it provided that the Association should instruct the publishing houses to include more local material in the textbooks. Primary school teachers were to form a society for the investigation and collection of material to be included in primary texts and there was also to be established a textbook-writing society from which textbook writers were to obtain suggestions. All publishers were to be kept informed as to what sort of texts primary school teachers wanted.[27] This was indeed a liberal and important development. During the debate a motion was presented that only national, as opposed to local, groups were to write primary textbooks, but it was rejected in favor of the former motion.[28]

As a result of the adoption of a system of education modelled upon the American "6-6-3" plan, in November, 1922, this conference devoted much time and effort to a revision of the curricula. American educational aims and ideals were to permeate the new system to a large degree as is strikingly seen in the development of the emphasis on civics readers and on citizenship. The aims of the new system were as follows:

1. To adapt itself to a changed and changing society.
2. To promote the spirit of democracy.
3. To develop individuality.
4. To take into special consideration the economic status of the average citizen.
5. To adjust education to the needs of life.
6. To facilitate the spread of universal education.
7. To make education flexible enough to allow for local variations.[29]

These aims of 1922 were in striking contrast with the earlier, vaguer, less liberal, and more militaristic aims hitherto set forth. They were indeed too liberal for the nationalistic China of 1925 and following, as the aims set forth by the

National Educational Conference of May, 1928, held under Kuomintang auspices at Nanking, and discussed below, will indicate. In fact these aims, and the whole new system, were drawn up and adopted without the sanction of the Ministry of Education, behind which were entrenched the politico-nationalistic forces. This was done by a group of professionally-minded educators, organized in their own associations, and carrying on in an environment sufficiently free of nationalists and politicians to enable them to work out their professional desires.[30]

The reorganized primary school curriculum followed, in general, that drawn up by a special committee appointed by the Conference of the Federation of Provincial Educational Associations "in collaboration with some leaders in elementary education in the province of Kiangsu, for long a source of new ideas in Chinese education." The group designated as "Social Study," which included hygiene, citizenship, geography and history, was to occupy 20 per cent of the time throughout the six years of the primary school. In the citizenship course the home was considered in the first year, followed in the second by general conditions of the school and the community; in the third year, the conditions in the district and the province; the fourth year the state and the responsibilities of national citizenship; in the fifth year the organization of the function of school and local government, and the citizen's responsibilities thereto, and finally the organization and function of the county, province, and state, and duties of the citizen thereto. In history the first four years were devoted to stories. In the third year the stress was to be on the life of primitive people, and of people in remote lands. In the fourth year the history of inventions was to be given, also the important events in modern Chinese history and the general conditions of the Chinese people. Further important events in Chinese history were to be studied in the fifth year and continued in the sixth, with the addition of a few important events in world history. It is noteworthy that even in this most liberal and advanced program there was little space given to the history of the world at large. In geography the fifth and sixth years were devoted to Chinese geography, with certain essentials of world geography added in the last year. Ten per cent of the time was devoted to physical culture. For the first time free play, in contrast with military drill and formal physical exercise, was provided for in all years. However "imitation drill" was included from the third year on.[31]

An example of the "new" civics readers for primary schools is given in the survey (Appendix I) below number XXV. The new national language readers were written after 1920 in the Mandarin vernacular rather than in the classical *Wen Li*. (See survey below numbers XXXVIII and XXXIX.) They may be contrasted with numbers XL and XLI, written after 1925, to show the extent to which the resurgent nationalistic spirit reflected itself in the readers. For an example of the new educational system geographies for primary schools see survey number XVII.

In the reorganized middle school of the "new" educational system the aim in the required courses was ". . . to safeguard the basis of effective democracy and social integration" by cultivating ". . . common feeling, common thought and common aspiration among the junior middle school students."[32]

Elective courses were offered to students to permit flexibility in meeting their varying needs. The course in civics was one of the "constants" or required courses. The term 'civics' is used in its broad sense, including not only a knowledge of social, governmental and economic order, but also that of character formation. It gives training in ethical judgment and attitude, as well as promoting the spirit of patriotic and social service. Besides, it also pays attention to international relationships. It aims to train students to be members of a home, of a community and citizens of a nation, who also appreciate the spirit of international democracy.[33]

The aims in teaching general history were as follows:

1. Cultivation in the students of the power of adjusting themselves to their environment through the study of evolution of the associated life of men.

2. Cultivation of "universal love" and the spirit of coöperation in students through the development of human sympathy.

3. Study of the cause and effect of past events in order to make students understand the truth concerning present affairs and enable them to seek solutions for modern social problems.

4. Guidance of the students constantly through the study of history, especially in its method, so as to develop their interest in, and to form the habit of, studying history.

The committee [appointed by the National Educational Association at its annual conference in October, 1922] deems it necessary to combine Chinese history and the history of the world into one course in the junior middle school, in order to make the students understand the evolution of the world's civilization as a whole. It will cultivate mutual understanding among nations, a sympathetic attitude toward international affairs, and an enlightened outlook on the world.[34]

The purposes of the required geography courses were:

1. To study the [relation] of man [to] nature, in order to enable the student to adjust himself to his physiographic, economic, social, and political environment; .

2. To explain to the student the real situation of economic interdependence among the nations, so as to develop international sympathy;

3. To tell students the position of China in the world, in order to cultivate the spirit of self-reliance and self-determination of a nation;

4. To lead [them] to a deep appreciation of the beauties of nature, so as to give [them] some aesthetic enjoyment.[35]

Foreign languages were required only of those students who planned to continue their education. For those intending to leave school at the end of junior middle school, vocational training was offered as a substitute for foreign language.[36]

For history textbooks, written and used, that embodied this advanced and liberal interpretation of the function of history teaching, see numbers VII to XI, inclusive, in Appendix I. For civics published and used that are in harmony with the above aims for that course see numbers XXII to XXVI. Contrast these better civics readers with the *San Min Chu I* readers which displaced them, for the most part, in the schools after 1928. The more important ones are reviewed in numbers XXVII to XXXII. The liberal aims outlined above find no place in these later texts. The geography texts which appeared after 1928 failed to meet the very high standard set for them above. (See numbers XLVI to XLVIII.)

In Shansi province, under the able and peaceful governorship of General Yen Hsi-shan during the years from 1916 to 1924, the educational system was developed to a degree scarcely equalled in any other province. It was there that modern civics textbooks were first used to any extent. The first was called *What a Citizen Ought to Know*. During 1918-1919 the provincial government printed and distributed

2,700,000 copies in the province. It contained chapters relating to the civic virtues of faithfulness, progressiveness, and patriotism; education; industries; the family; society; nationality, with topics on the national flag and anthem and one chapter on the world in general.[37]

Following the Shanghai and Canton incidents of May and June 1925 a wave of nationalistic fervor and indignation swept the nation. It was immediately reflected in educational circles. At educational conferences that followed, pleas were made and motions passed favouring a more nationalistic type of education. This we have already noted above.[38] Scores of articles appeared in the educational journals advocating a revision of educational aims and of textbooks, to be in harmony with this emotion of resentment and humiliation aroused by contact with foreigners and their imperialistic forces. The Chung Hwa Press, always ardently nationalistic, promoted nationalism through its *Educational Review*. Two special numbers in July and August of that year were devoted to the subject. Every phase of the educational system was written upon by a score or more of writers aiming further to nationalize education. One of these articles on "The Question of Nationalism and Middle School Citizenship Teaching" by Li Kuan-ch'ing indicates the general temper of the new movement in education especially as applying to the civics readers, the development of which, to 1925, has been traced above.[39]

Mr. Li advocated that education for citizenship be made the prime aim and motivating center for all other phases of the educational system. Granting that the idea of citizenship was one that extended from the family and village through the nation to the world, he asserted that in order to make it real and vital for this stage of the world's development educators must emphasize the nationalistic type of citizen above all others. The chief end, as he defined it, of citizenship was to make the nation strong and independent. It is true, he pointed out, that since the World War there had been a strong peace movement, still he held it to be apparent that imperialistic forces were yet in existence, and that the only way to world peace was through building up strong nations. Therefore, he concluded, the movement for citizenship education should be intimately identified with the "National Salvation" movement. The aims in the courses on citizenship should be to show clearly how the interests of the nation and the people were one and the same and thereby cause to flourish the spirit of patriotism; to create in the people a willingness to sacrifice all for the nation and to show them the necessity for supporting the "National Salvation Movement."

The attack upon the civics readers continued for months in this same educational review. In December of 1926 a special number on Citizenship appeared. One of the leading articles by Wen Tien, "A Criticism of the Citizenship Creed" took exception to the citizenship creed adopted by the Kiangsu Provincial Educational Association, as not being in harmony with the newer nationalistic educational aims. In order to bring out the type of creed which he thought China should have he compared it with the more highly nationalistic citizenship creed used in America, quoting patriotic statements of E. E. Hale, Jefferson, Madison, Webster and Lincoln. He asserted that the creeds of other countries were similar to that of America. The Kiangsu creed he criticized as being too vague and universal in its implications.

This same educational review under the editorship of

Ch'ên Ch'i-t'ien, an ardent nationalist, devoted a special number in July, 1926 to the question of patriotic material in primary school courses. The writers for the number advocated the introduction of more material designed to arouse the patriotism of the students into the following textbooks: readers, civics, history, geography, social science and even arithmetic and drawing.

These ardent nationalistic philosopher-educators attained their goal with a rapidity and thoroughness that must have exceeded their fondest hopes. With the advent to power of the nationalist party after 1927 the educational aims, curricula, and textbooks were revised in accordance with the most advanced form of modern nationalism. Mr. Wong Yun-wu, editor-in-chief of the Commercial Press, told the writer in a personal interview that the civics readers were being rapidly displaced by the new *San Min Chu I* readers which incorporate the doctrines and philosophies of the Kuomintang party. Mr. Lofee Pahong, formerly general manager of the Chung Hua Press in an interview said, that the sale of civics readers had fallen off 40 per cent since the publication of the *San Min Chu I* readers. The sale of the latter had already by the spring of 1929 doubled that of the former. He thought these texts were not so good as the civic readers. Moreover, they were very difficult to write. A little too much emphasis in one direction, he said, led to Communism, and in the other direction to Imperialism. The sale of the old *hsiu shên,* or ethical culture, readers declined considerably in both presses, though the Commercial Press reported a sale of over 50,000 sets a year. For a comparison in the spirit and content of the new *San Min Chu I* texts and the civics readers see Appendix I. The former texts are much more nationalistic than the latter.

The *San Min Chu I* texts are striking in their lack of the conception of citizenship, and fail to show to the child his relation to the home, the family, and the community and to the international society. Nationalistic political thought predominates and all problems and relationships of life are seen from the national viewpoint. The heroes resurrected as models for the students to emulate are always of a nationalistic and often militaristic type. This applies to the new national readers as well. As late as the spring of 1929, the textbooks on history and geography had not been rewritten to bring them into harmony with the aims and spirit of the Nationalist government. One exception to this is seen in the history text reviewed below (number XIII). National economic policies are now in the process of formulation. The possible effect of these on textbooks is evidenced in an order issued by the Bureau of Commercial and Industrial Information of the Ministry of Industry, Commerce and Labor in coöperation with the Ministry of Education to all provincial educational departments and muncipal educational bureaus to compile textbooks for middle and primary schools including a full description of China's leading industries and stories to arouse interest in them.[40]

In the survey of textbooks used in the primary and middle schools of China, from the time when the first modern system of education was adopted in 1903 to the present, the aim has been to note the attitude toward the nation which the educators have attempted to instill into the youths. For that reason the textbooks on ethics, the readers, history, and geography, together with the mass education readers have been examined. About forty-eight sets are summarized in the Appendix, though the author has examined a score more. It will be noted that practically all of these textbooks were published by the Commercial and the Chung Hua Presses. Estimating conservatively, these two houses publish about 70 per cent of the texts used in the schools, and, furthermore, set the standard for the many small presses that supply the remainder. For that reason, together with the fact that the texts chosen were those having the highest sale, the author feels he has made a fair survey. The repeated changes in the form and content of the texts is in close harmony with the changing educational aims and curricula of the educational system and this in turn is intimately related to the fluctuating political history of the nation during the past thirty years. It was a period of rapid change and the presses were repeatedly compelled to rewrite the textbooks to meet the changing demands of the groups of educators and politicians who chanced to be in office. Needless to say these texts will be revised if the political wheel again turns, but there is one permanent and even increasing tendency in all this flux: this is that modern education in China is conceived of as a legitimate and proper tool of the state for indoctrinating the students in the spirit and principles of modern nationalism. This tendency gives little promise of abatement unless international relations materially improve and educators in the leading nations coöperate to rewrite educational aims and textbooks with a view toward ushering in a harmoniously conceived world community.

CHAPTER V

NATIONALISM IN MODERN CHINA

Modern nationalism may be defined as the creation, through press, societies, the platform, and the school, among all or nearly all the members of a nationality, a self-conscious attitude toward their common linguistic, cultural, and historical heritage *together with* the arousing of a sense of patriotism demanding a supreme loyalty to the political State.[1] It is the union of these two sentiments that makes for what we call modern nationalism. The first of these the Chinese have long had; indeed, one may note its clear emergence in the writings of China's Classical Age from the fifth to the third centuries before Christ. We find there a keen awareness of the peculiar virtues and the inherent excellence of their own culture. This self-consciousness arose from continuous contact with "barbarian" tribes throughout the long centuries. In modern times, during the two hundred and fifty and more years they were under the alien rule of the Manchus, this self-conscious spirit of racial and cultural superiority was intensified, especially in the provinces south of the Yangtze, where secret societies from time to time agitated for the overthrow of the Ch'ing and the restoration of the preceding native or Ming dynasty.

Patriotic and loyal devotion to the conception of an abstract sovereign state did not exist until after the establishment of the Republic, and even today it has not permeated much beyond restricted intellectual circles.[2] What patriotism there existed under the Manchu régime was confined to the literati and the official classes, in the time-honored Confucian sense of the supremacy of the five social relationships, the first of which demanded loyalty to the Emperor. This loyalty, however, was never absolute in form, being suffused and tempered by the rich social, pragmatic and relativistic coloring which all Chinese thought carries. The Emperor was held to rule by mandate from Heaven in behalf of, and for the welfare of, the people. This left the way open for revolution if the dynasty failed to bring the people comfort and peace. Then too, this relationship was only one of the five relationships. Man's duty to his parents being second in importance and at all times and in all events this was the most real and vital relationship for the majority of the people. Indeed Hsien Fêng, who ruled from 1850-61, is reported to have exclaimed when so many officials were resigning to attend to family affairs during the T'aip'ing Rebellion, that his people were more loyal to their families than to him. This loyalty of the Chinese toward their family, village, district and province, superseding that of loyalty to the Sovereign, has been a marked characteristic. Foreigners in China during the nineteenth century repeatedly pointed to the fact and attributed China's weakness and lack of unity primarily to it.[3]

In the latter half of the nineteenth century a few Chinese intellectuals in close touch with the foreigners apparently caught the idea of modern national patriotism from them and commenced to propagate it among others of their own class. From the intellectuals it spread to the commercial classes and later to the laborers and, to a much lesser extent, to the peasants. K'ang Yu-wei, the outstanding intellectual reformer at the close of the century, wrote repeatedly on Japanese patriotism recounting to his many eager readers how the Japanese, imbued with an ardent patriotism, had unified their empire and brought it out of feudalism, and had modernized and strengthened it.[4] Liang Ch'i-ch'ao, his brilliant disciple, took upon himself the task of arousing the people to this spirit of nationalism, as he conceived it, as the one way in which to preserve the Chinese race. As he wrote at one time and reiterated again and again in numerous articles, "The world of today is a world of racialism. Any country that wishes to establish itself certainly must have its peculiar characteristics, have its own geographical area, its own history, its own thought, and its own customs."[5] He had much to say about the nature and value of patriotism.[6] These two men were outstanding leaders in the development of modern nationalism in China. While not strictly nationalists in the modern sense they did much to bring before the people the necessity for reform if the Chinese race and culture were to survive in a world of rapacious nations.

So deeply stirred was Liang by the perilous situation in which his country was placed by the aggressive West that he sought to reinterpret the whole of Confucian philosophy in order to emphasize its militaristic aspects and thereby strengthen his people and give them the will to fight for the nation. "How does it happen," he asks, "though Christianity and Buddhism both teach love and gentleness yet their followers are filled with lust for fighting, while the followers of Confucius are not militaristic?" The reason is that the milder virtues have been over-emphasized by the interpreters of Confucianism, though in the Sage's writings are passages extolling the sterner virtues of the fight. "In place of emphasizing the joy of strength and the bravery of danger they have made submissiveness the greatest good. . . . To live with such an attitude of submissiveness in the modern world," he says, "is as though when a strong thief breaks into your house and places a knife at your throat, you argue with him over the meaning of good and evil."[7]

The rapidly rising Chinese press, after 1895, was predominantly patriotic in tone.[8] It was the chief medium, apart from the educational system, through which the early nationalist reformers worked. This patriotic press in the hands of reformers such as Liang, had an indirect influence in molding the spirit and aims of the first established system of modern education. Of more direct influence was the collection of essays edited by Viceroy Chang Chih-tung and called "An Exhortation to Study." It appeared in the spring of 1898 and attained, under Imperial sanction, a circulation of over a million copies. The first five essays therein are devoted to an exposition of the kind of nationalistic spirit held to be desirable by this reforming official and his associates. As he was one of the commission of three that established the first modern educational system in 1903 it might be well to quote his summary in the preface of these five papers.[9]

1. Unite your hearts. It is clear that the protection of your country, the protection of your religion and the protection of your race is one and the same idea. . . .
2. Teach loyalty [to the nation]. From the reigning dynasty you have obtained many blessings. Therefore, all officials and

people should cherish the utmost sentiments of loyalty toward it in order to protect the country.

3. Clarify the fundamental principles . . . in order to protect the national doctrine [Confucianism].

4. Know your [racial] characteristics . . . in order to protect your race.

5. Pay due reverence to the Classics. . . .

The relation of the growing conception of modern nationalism to the changing educational aims and curricula has been followed in some detail in the preceding chapters. Of outstanding interest was the marked change after 1925 when the spirit and philosophy of modern nationalism rapidly developed in influence, thoroughly permeating the educational aims and curricula from that time to the present. The effect on the educational system has been noted above. In order to gain a clearer conception of the nature and quality of this spirit significant portions of the writings of a number of outstanding educators, as well as of Sun Yat-sen will be briefly summarized. This spirit may then be profitably contrasted with Chang Chih-tung's conception of nationalism as set forth above.

Mr. Ch'ên Ch'i-t'ien, editor of the *Chung Hua Educational Review,* is an ardent nationalist. In his magazine innumerable articles appeared, many of them from his pen, setting forth the philosophy of modern nationalism as developed in the West, together with plans and methods whereby it might be introduced into the curricula and textbooks of the school system. He attended the fourth annual conference of the Association for the Advancement of Education in 1925, where he was primarily instrumental in securing the passage of a motion revising the educational aims so as to conform to the idea of nationalism. The western sources of his nationalistic thought are indicated in an article written for the *New Education* in February 1924.[10] His article was based in part on Professor Edward H. Reisner's book, *Nationalism and Education since 1789*. From it many quotations were drawn. Ch'ên pointed out that education was the privilege and duty of the state and he was, therefore, opposed to all education on the part of religious groups. He deplored the universal and denationalized educational aims of the period prior to 1925 and, as has been noted above, was instrumental in bringing about a change by taking advantage of the spirit of resentment and hatred induced by the May 30th incident (1925). To support his argument he drew upon an article of Liang Ch'i-ch'ao's appearing in the *Hsin Min Pao* in 1902, called a "Discussion on Fixing Suitable Educational Aims."[11] In this article Liang stated that education should be the tool of the people in reconstructing the nation. The educators should first determine what are the nation's peculiar characteristics and then proceed to define the educational aims accordingly.

In September, 1924, Mr. Ch'ên wrote in the *Chung Hua Educational Review* an article called, "The New Nationalism and the Reconstruction of National Education." (*Hsin Kuo Chia Chu I Yü Kuo Min Chiao Yü Ti Kai Tsao*). He opposed post-war idealism and internationalism, stating that China must first of all be nationalized. He advocated the inclusion of more nationalistic materials in textbooks; but disapproved of the use of foreign languages in primary schools as hindering the natural development of the nation's peculiar characteristics. He asserted that in history texts material promoting love of the fatherland should be added and that

emphasis should be placed on the national indignities suffered at the hands of westerners.

In the same magazine for October, 1926, Mr. Ch'ên outlined a policy for Chinese governmental education (*Chung
Kuo Chiao Yü Chêng Ts'ê*). He repeatedly denounced the
desire of certain educators for educational independence or
freedom from political and party control. He was, however,
an ardent opponent of educational control and influence
coming from without the nation. The policy he advocated
at that time was two-fold: first to spread the knowledge of
the "nation's shame" as a means of arousing the people to
coöperate in national salvation, and secondly to recover the
educational prerogatives. The methods of carrying out this
policy were outlined as follows: firstly, revise the educational aims and see that they are carried out; secondly, carefully supervise all education by private groups and individ-
uals; thirdly, prevent education by missionary societies;
fourthly, prevent the colonial educational policies of the
Japanese in Shantung and Manchuria and Russians in Outer
Mongolia; fifthly, promote military training in the schools;
sixthly, promote education among Chinese emigrants; sev-
enthly, exploit energetically frontier education among Tibetans, Mongolians, Miaotze, etc.

The general question of nationalism and its relation to
education was widely and enthusiastically discussed in the
Chung Hua Educational Review, the July and August numbers of 1925 being devoted especially to the subject. One of
the articles discussed the relation of education and nationalism to individualism, cosmopolitanism, and democracy.[12] The
author attempted first of all to show that individualism and
nationalism were not opposing ideas. He quoted Sheridan,

Fichte, Hegel, and others in support of his contention that there can be "self-realization through state service." He opposed cosmopolitanism as being antithetical to nationalism. Nationalism and democracy he held not to be antithetical ideas as seen in the Americanization programs of the United States. He pointed out that the national body was one in which all classes should coöperate and, therefore, class war should not be tolerated. He quoted Fichte to the effect that all the members of a state form one living organic body.

Other articles in special numbers of the *Chung Hua Educational Review* dealt with the relation of nationalism to education in France, England, Germany and the United States. There were also articles on the relation of nationalism to ethics and to citizenship; of its place in primary, middle and normal schools and its bearing on military drill and physical education. One of the articles by Fan Yüan-lien,[13] sometime Minister of Education and an outstanding educational leader, set forth the substance of a speech which he made just after the May and June incidents of 1925. He stated in substance that what China needed was not educational internationalism, localism, or socialism, but educational nationalism. All the countries since the war have been emphasizing that type of education. Referring to the Shanghai incident he said that a common spirit of coöperation should result from it. A National Educational Union was organized at this time with the avowed purpose of nationalizing the educational system.

That Chiang Monlin, Minister of Education from 1928 to 1930, is a modern nationalist will be seen in the following quotations from his book, *A Study in the Chinese Principles of Education*. He advocated therein the so-called German view that the State should dominate all human affairs as ". . . in view of the practical, social, and national demands of the time, the Chinese people must realize that in this stage of international strife for power, they must sacrifice their individual inclinations for the national good. . . ." The people should realize that

during the coming hundred years, their devotion to the state is absolutely necessary for their political independence, which is the foundation for the future national culture, and they not only owe themselves the full development of their native pow- ers . . . but also their national consciousness which is funda- mental to patriotism. And patriotism is the chief virtue of a people who love political freedom. . . . Patriotism is demanded of the people by themselves for the protection of their political freedom, and it is the spirit of national defense. . . . National defense and national culture form the vital issue of China's national problem. This is at the same time the problem of na- tional education of the young Republic, for national education is a means of solving national problems. . . . If the citizen has the right to demand from the state protection and assistance, the state has also the right to make demands upon the citizen for his defense of his country, and devotion to her. Citizenship implies both rights and duties. Nobody can enjoy rights per- manently without the fulfillment of duties. Therefore Patriot- ism is the supreme virtue of citizenship.[14]

Ts'ai Yüan-p'ei, twice Minister of Education and now director of the Academia Sinica is more explicit with respect to the duties which a citizen owes his state. Among others he has emphasized the duty of all citizens becoming soldiers that a militaristic state might be created.[15] This is quite in harmony with his previous statements on the subject.[16]

The Mass Education Movement is nationalistic in spirit and method, but mildly so. For a survey of its textbooks see the digest (in Appendix I) below, numbers I to VI. The leader of the movement, Y.C. James Yen, is an humanitarian nationalist. He wrote at the time when the movement was being launched as follows:

Is it mere accident that China is preserved through all these centuries, while other republics and empires of equally noble history have fallen and gone? Is it mere accident that China has the greatest and most homogeneous people on the face of the globe? No, it cannot be! Quite on the contrary, we are all convinced, China has a mission toward the war-torn world, and that mission, we believe, is to teach it the way of peace. She loves peace, and the world has jeered at her for it. She was once the teacher of Asia, the cradle of the world's civilization. [sic] She began practising democracy centuries before the discovery of the world's greatest republic, the United States of America. Such a great past deserves a great future.[17]

Again he writes, ". . . through a common effort to advance a common cause such as that championed by the Mass Education Movement, China can be molded into one united nation." He continues by stating that the movement aims at training for true citizenship, at unifying the nation and then working for the realization of world peace.[18] In the eight years or more since its inception the movement has taught perhaps a million illiterates the elements of reading. It aimed at one time to teach the hundred million or more younger adults to read. In recent years it has concentrated its activities on building up a model district at *Ting Hsien* where not only the language is taught but improved agricultural and stock-raising methods as well. The fact that its leader and many of his colleagues were educated in Christian schools, together with the fact that it has successfully appealed to the American public for funds tends to give the movement a certain humanitarian air and to prevent it to the present from becoming intolerantly nationalistic and anti-foreign. However, it is interesting to note that the only references in the movement's textbooks to the world, apart from China, were (in 1929) adverse and critical comments on the foreign merchants in Chinese territory.

It has already been noted that the present Kuomintang government decided in its first national educational conference held in May, 1928, to call its type of education *San Min Chu I* education.[19] It aimed to educate in the spirit of the "Three Principles of the People" as propounded by the party's founder and leader Dr. Sun Yat-sen.[20] How these principles are now being presented to the primary and middle school students may be seen in the digest of textbooks below, numbers XXVII-XXXII, XL-XLI. Dr. Sun in the preface to his published lectures on the three principles wrote, "I hope that all our comrades will take the book as a basis or as a stimulus, expand and correct it, supply omissions, improve the arrangement and make it a perfect text for propaganda purposes."[21] Variations of interpretation and emphasis could be made without number or restraint, the very vagueness and inclusiveness of the principles make for misunderstanding.

As the translator states in his preface, *Min-ts'u,* for example, was used by Dr. Sun in the sense of "nation," "nationality," or "race," depending upon the context. *Min-ch'üan* sometimes means "sovereignty," sometimes "rights," and at other times "power" or "authority."[22]

Excerpts taken from the text of the *Principles* will best serve to illustrate the quality of the spirit of nationalism and the attitude toward, and conception of, the state which animates them. The three principles of the people are ". . .

the principles of our nation's salvation." Their aim is to ". . . elevate China to an equal position among the nations in international affairs, in government, and in economic life, so that she can permanently exist in the world."[23] Dr. Sun asserted that the Chinese nationality or race is coterminous with the state or nation, and contrasted China in this respect with the British Empire. But he stated there has been no nationalism in China. The unity of the Chinese people has stopped short at the clan. There follows a long discussion of the old-fashioned five-colored-races-of-the-world idea. He concluded,

Considering the law of the survival of ancient and modern races, if we want to save China and to preserve the Chinese race, we must certainly promote Nationalism. [Apart from some ten millions of alien races in China] . . . the Chinese people are of the Han or Chinese race with common blood, common language, common religion and common customs. . . . But the Chinese people have only family and clan groups; there is no national spirit. . . . We are the poorest and weakest state in the world . . . our position is now extremely perilous. If we do not earnestly promote nationalism and weld together our four hundred million into a strong nation, we face a tragedy, the loss of our country and the destruction of our race. To ward off this danger, we must espouse Nationalism and employ the national spirit to save the country.[24]

He said the Chinese incline too easily toward a spirit of cosmopolitanism. "Those young students who prate about the new culture and espouse cosmopolitanism, saying that nationalism is out of date, might have some ground if they spoke for England and America, or even for our fore-fathers, but if they think they are speaking for Chinese today, we have no place for them." China must first make itself into a strong state and then there may be talk of cosmopolitanism or internationalism.[25] This internationalism has only just appeared in Europe during this generation, but it was talked of two thousand years ago in China and it was based on a pacifist morality.[26] ". . . I think that in the relation between the citizens of China and their state, there must be family loyalty, then clan loyalty, and finally national loyalty."[27]

In order to recover the national spirit it is necessary to revive both the old learning and the old morality. "China's ancient virtues of loyalty, filial devotion, kindness, love, faithfulness and such are in their very nature superior to foreign virtues, but in the moral quality of Peace we will further surpass the people of other lands."[28]

Concerning the reasons for the espousal of democracy Sun says, "Thirty years ago [c. 1894], therefore, we fellow revolutionaries firmly resolved that, if we wanted China to be strong and our revolution to be effective, we must espouse the cause of democracy."[29] Further on he said, ". . . we in our revolution have chosen democracy, first, that we may be following the world tendency, and secondly, that we may reduce the period of civil war."[30] Democracy was to be a means of destroying Imperial ambitions and of uniting the nation. The third principle was defined as ". . . the People's Livelihood. It denotes the livelihood of the people, the existence of society, the welfare of the nation, the life of the masses. . . . The principle of livelihood is socialism, it is communism, it is utopianism."[31]

NATIONALIST SYMBOLS

Wherever there is a nationalistic state there exist national songs and a national flag to symbolize its spirit. China proves no exception to this rule. At an early date Chinese nationalists, seeing the existence of these symbols elsewhere, felt that they should have them and set about consciously to create them. In February, 1913, the Ministry of Education sent a letter to Liang Ch'i-ch'ao asking him to compose a national song suitable for the new Republic. It pointed out that the purpose of such a song was to unify the people, who were to sing it upon all public occasions. In the Educational Conference of the preceding summer the problem was raised and discussed. It was decided to ask men of literary ability to compose one. Since that time over three hundred songs had been received, but not one was felt to be suitable. The Ministry hoped that Liang would present one. Along with the letter summarized above, a copy of a number of translated national songs of other nations was sent by way of suggestion.[32]

In May, 1913, seven songs were selected by the Ministry and presented to the President for his selection. The communication stated,

The civilized nations of the world all have national songs which they use on ceremonial occasions. It represents the consciousness of nationality. China should have one, not simply because other nations have, but because it is most natural to have one. . . . If we do not have a national song we cannot show our national spirit to other countries nor can we reconcile the spirit of the five races that comprise the Republic.[33]

All the drafts were redolent of the spirit of nationalism and of patriotic sentiment. The song selected was an adaptation of a very old one and was called the "Song of the Green Clouds." It may be translated as follows: "The Chinese five-coloured flag is like the rainbow in the clouds which

sparkles colorfully in the sky. China is like the sun and the
moon waxing and waning endlessly day by day." Yüan
Shih-k'ai no doubt selected this least offensive of the seven
that foreign powers, whom he ardently wooed for financial
reasons, might not become offended. In 1921 the music for
the song was rewritten in the form in which it exists today.
It was a matter of great importance and was discussed by
the Cabinet before being approved by the President. Then
it was communicated by the Ministry of Education to all
military and provincial governors throughout the nation.[34]

The five-barred and colored flag, one color for each of
the five races of the nation, was adopted upon the establishment of the Republic. It was decreed by the Senate in
June, 1912. A communication sent by the Ministry of Education to the Ministry of the Interior requested it to order
local authorities to see that each family had a national
flag and that it be displayed on ceremonial days and holidays. "The national flag is the symbol of the whole nation
in the eyes of the world. Within the country it reflects the
spirit of the citizens. Therefore, in the modern world there
is no one who does not respect his particular national flag and
hold it to be the evidence of the nation's spirit. They consider the flag as important as life itself." The life of a people
depends upon the nation and the flag represents to them the
symbol of their livelihood. "However, there still remain
many people, especially in the villages and towns, whose
conception of the national flag is not clear and who do not
understand its significance." Therefore, the Ministry of Interior ordered all policemen to see that each family had a
national flag and that it was displayed on national holidays.

The order concluded that if the people pay respect to the flag it will call forth in them the sentiment of patriotism.[35]

In pursuance of this order one of the lectures prepared by the Popular Educational Association at Peking was on the National Flag. A portion of it will be given here:[36]

Countrymen, do you see the flag which hangs before every public office? This is our national flag . . . every independent nation has a national flag, and every national flag has a meaning.

Our national flag has five colors: red, yellow, blue, white, and black; each representing one part of our country. . . . It has an ethical meaning. The five colors represent five virtues: benevolence, righteousness, harmony, wisdom and honesty.

A national flag is to represent a nation. . . . The national flag to a nation is just as a signboard to a store. The signboard of a store is very important (to the Chinese mind at least). If you destroy it that store will bring suit against you. If you do not pay respect to a national flag it means that you do not respect that nation. Remember, countrymen, the Opium War was begun by not paying respect to the flag of Great Britain, and the result was China was forced to open five ports for foreign trade.

So we must not only pay respect to our national flag, but also to the flags of other nations.

With the rise of the Kuomintang to power the five-colored flag has been lowered and the Kuomintang flag, a white-starred sun on a blue field, has been adopted in its stead as the national flag of China. In one room, at least, of all schools and official bureaus, it is required that a picture of Sun Yat-sen be hung, and draped with flags. Below or beside his picture his will is also shown. Once a week in the schools and at every official gathering respectful bows are made to the picture and the will is read. In the school service, songs are sung and usually a talk is given by some local politician on the Three Principles of the People or on some phase of the party platform. In all of these ways, as well as in the more formal schooling, the spirit of modern nationalism and of loyalty to a party and the nation is artificially and consciously stimulated. In the absence of a new national song the Kuomintang has adopted its own party anthem. On January 10th, 1929, at Nanking, it was adopted by a standing committee of the central executive committee. The words were written by Dr. Sun Yat-sen and the music composed by a Professor Chêng Mou-chün of the Central University. Several compositions were submitted to a special committee including General Chiang Kai-shek, chairman of the national government; Mr. Hu Han-min, chairman of the legislative yuan; Mr. Tai Chi-t'ao, chairman of the examination yuan; Mr. Ts'ai Yüan-p'ei, chairman of the control yuan; and Mr. Chiang Mon-lin, Minister of Education. The following translation of the songs brings out the exact meaning of the Chinese words, without regard to rhyme or syllables:—

> *San Min Chu I,*
> Our Party's aim,
> To rebuild the Republic
> And establish Universal Brotherhood [Ta T'ung]
>
> Press on, comrades,
> Vanguard of the people!
> Cease not your vigil,
> But ever follow the Principles!
>
> Be diligent, be brave,
> Be true, be loyal,
> With one heart, one mind,
> Carry through to the end.[37]

The Literary Revolution, Nationalism and Modern Education

The relation between the conception of universal compulsory education, of democracy, of modern nationalism, and of the rise of the use of the vernacular languages in the various nations as the medium of literary expression is now so inextricably interwoven that only the most careful research can unravel them and give to each its due place and emphasis. In China these four elements have but recently become correlated harmoniously into the evolved educational system of a modern universal, nationalistic type using the most widely spoken language as the medium of literary expression. And that system affects now some 15 to 20 per cent of the school population of the country. This all came about during the years 1895 to 1925. In Europe the same development took between three and four centuries. The Chinese after 1895, began to realize that the power and unity existing within western nations and in Japan was due to the use of this type of education. They commenced consciously to adopt it. The stimulus behind it, which at all times carried the reforms of the bolder, more progressive leaders to a successful fruition, was the deep-felt necessity for preserving the national culture and the political integrity of the nation in the face of the ruthless imperialism of the western nations and of Japan. This deep-felt emotion was the main-spring of all action on the part of reformers in the government as well as in the educational field. The repeated expressions of this emotion have been noted above in the educational field. It was, at first, a more or less spontaneous reaction to foreign encroachment, and gradually became, as we have seen, transformed into a conscious, dogmatic belief exhibiting many of the characteristics of a religion with all the appropriate creeds, symbols, and hymns that religions commonly possess. The school came to be the chief vehicle for transmitting this orthodox sentiment to the youth and, as will be pointed out below, its successful rise was marked by the almost complete elimination of all competing religious instructions—Confucian, Buddhist, Christian or Mohammedan, from established schools.

The final adoption of the vernacular, or *pai hua,* as the means of instruction in the primary schools has been immediately attributed to the success of the Nationalist Student Movement of 1919. A history of that development will be of interest to reveal what influence the rising spirit of nationalism had upon it. Toward the close of the nineteenth century a few Chinese reformers felt the need of simplifying the classical *wên li* in order to carry western thought and science to a greater number of people. Chang Chih-tung, in one of his memorials advocating administrative reform suggested, as one of the twelve ways in which to bring about desirable change, the elimination of classical phraseology and allusions, so that a simple clear literary style might develop.[38] It has already been noted that one of the outstanding characteristics of Liang Ch'i-ch'ao's writing was the new forceful and trenchant style which he developed. He consciously used it and advocated its use.[39] But more than this was demanded, after 1917, by extreme reformers. A number of papers and periodicals commenced to be published in *pai hua,* or the Mandarin vernacular.[40] The feeling among these intellectuals was that in order to save China they must do something for the people. "We can do nothing without the people, we are nothing ourselves. Such were the desires that one could very often read in the journals [of the period after

1895]."[41] Hence the necessity for writing in a language
which the people could more readily understand. For centuries, especially since the Yüan dynasty, novels, dramas,
and romantic histories had been appearing in the Northern
vernacular. Even before Yüan the great T'ang poets wrote in
a simplified style as did the renowned Sung philosopher, Chu
Hsi. In the Ch'ing dynasty the commentary on the Sacred
Edict was in Mandarin. The translation of the Bible into
Kuan-hua, or Mandarin, in the latter half of the nineteenth
century no doubt also had some influence on the movement.
By the close of the Manchu dynasty such an extensive literature had developed that popular novels such as "The Dream
of the Red Chamber" were read everywhere—even in Canton where the dialect is much different from the *Kuan-hua* or
Mandarin dialect.[42] The use of this well-developed medium
of literary expression for spreading western thought and science and arousing the people to the spirit of reform, while
started soon after 1895, did not achieve success until after
1915.

Meanwhile the movement "to unify the national (spoken)
language" had arisen and the formulation of a national phonetic alphabet was undertaken. The more conservative officials took part in this movement and it was actively sponsored
by the Ministry of Education. Regardless which literary style
was employed, the value of formulating, for the spoken
language, a series of phonetic symbols to be placed beside the
characters as an aid to teaching the "national language" became apparent to conservatives as well as radicals.[43] In the
latter half of the nineteenth century Protestant missionaries
had Romanized several dialects and had published Biblical
literature in them.[44] In Japan the *Kana* or phonetic alphabet

was being effectively used to teach the language. In China the movement to phoneticize the *Kuan-hua* [after 1910 called the *kuo-yu,* or national language, to relieve it of the odium of the old name "official language,"[45]] was carried on also as a means of unifying the spoken language throughout the country. This was believed to be fundamentally essential to the unification of the country. As one of the leaders in the movement later said, the consummation of the movement would greatly facilitate the conduct of naval and army maneuvers on a nation-wide scale with dispatch.[46]

Some progress was made toward creating such an alphabet under the Imperial régime, but the present alphabet had its origin in the Conference for the Unification of the National Language held in Peking in 1913. An alphabet of thirty-nine symbols was created, but not officially adopted until November, 1918.[47] A year later a dictionary based on this phonetic alphabet was adopted. Meanwhile in 1916 in Peking there was created a Society for the Study of National Language Unification with representatives from each province. In the summer of 1917 the Board of Education appointed a man to go to Japan to investigate the methods employed by the Japanese to unify their national language. In 1918 the National Higher Normal School Principals' Conference adopted a resolution to establish national language practice courses in order to train teachers in the national phonetic alphabet.[48]

The movement to unify the national spoken language, while it had in the period prior to 1919 become well-established, did not make much popular headway until after that year, when it was officially ordered to be taught in the schools. On the other hand, the vernacular movement, which had for its purpose the popularization of the common language as the medium for literary expression, did not make much progress until 1915. About this time the younger generation of modern intellectuals, who, lacking sympathy for the older mandarinate and literati, commenced to make their influence felt. The movement centered at the National University of Peking where President Ts'ai Yüan-p'ei gave it his support. A number of the Professors including Hu Shih, Ch'ên Tu-hsiu, Chou Tso-jên, and others commenced to publish articles advocating the use of the vernacular language in such magazines as the *New Youth*, and the *Renaissance*.[40]

There was much serious opposition to their efforts. Yet there were many, especially in educational circles, who advocated the use of the vernacular. For example, as early as 1917 the National Federation of Educational Associations adopted a resolution to the effect that in the people's schools the national literature courses should be changed to national language courses.[50] The Ministry of Education, however, could not endorse such a radical departure at that time. At a National Language Unification Conference held in April of 1919 Hu Shih, Chou Tso-jên and others succeeded in passing a motion stating that the best way to promote the use of the national language was to change the primary-school textbooks from national literature readers to national language readers.[51]

Just after the close of this conference the Student Movement of 1919 took place, following reception of the news of the failure of the Peace Conference to return Shantung to China. The struggle against the pro-Japanese officials in power at Peking, who gave indication that they would sign the Versailles treaty, centered in the National University.

The students and their leaders were finally successful in keeping the government from signing the Versailles treaty and in securing the dismissal of three of the ministers.

This struggle, which lasted several months, made the National University exceedingly popular throughout the country, and the few new publications conducted by its professors and students were widely read and discussed. Realizing the importance of the literary and intellectual revolution already begun by the National University, the great political parties, the Kuomintang and the Chin-pu Tang, now cast their lot with the new movements and rivaled each other in converting their party organs into propaganda for what they understood as the "New Culture Movement."[52]

Some four hundred periodicals quickly sprang up, most of them in the vernacular. After 1919, however, the number shrank to about one hundred.

Taking that mass of magazines as a whole, one may roughly estimate the number of original articles therein contained to be forty per cent, translation or adaptations forming the remaining sixty per cent. Only about ten per cent of the articles are of a scientific nature, about forty per cent are purely literary, mostly short stories and poetry; and practically fifty per cent of the total is devoted to philosophical, ethical and political discussions of a rather general and popular nature.[53]

The prevailing tone of most of these magazines was nationalistic. Their purpose was to arouse the Chinese people to an awareness of their danger both from within and without, and to convince them of the necessity for modernizing their social, economic and political life.[54]

The rapid spread of the vernacular movement after May, 1919 culminated in a resolution passed by the delegates at the annual conference of Provincial Educational Associations asking the Minister of Education to order all the lower primary schools to use *pai hua* textbooks and all higher primary schools to use both *pai hua* and the easy classical *wen li*. In January of 1920 the Ministry ordered that beginning in the fall of that year *pai hua* textbooks should be used in the first two years of the primary school.[55] The tendency since has been to teach less and less in the *wen li*, in both primary and middle schools.

By way of conclusion, it may be stated that the leaders effective in raising the vernacular language to a form of literary expression, while doing it for certain democratic reasons as a means for carrying out universal and compulsory education were, with few exceptions, nationalists, whose primary aim was to use education as a tool for strengthening the industrial and political life of the nation; and as we have seen, it was a nationalist movement which popularized the *pai hua* movement and brought it to an earlier success than its leaders had dared hope. Democratic and universal education was conceived, developed and is now controlled by Chinese nationalists for the purpose of creating a strong national state.

NATIONALISM AND RELIGIOUS EDUCATION

The rise of national sentiment in China has been paralleled by an increasing opposition to, and official regulation of, the propagation of Confucianism, Buddhism, and Christianity in the schools. In the Republican Constitutions religious liberty "within the limits of the laws"[56] was always granted. Such regulations were, after 1918, to be especially directed against Christianity—Buddhist and Confucianist teachings having meanwhile been suppressed—in order to prevent the propagation of westernized Christianity at the expense of nationalism in the schools.

The problem of the control of Buddhism, in modern times, was never a serious one. Under the last dynasty Buddhism was well under the control of the State. Evidence has been given above of the willingness of the government to order Buddhist temples to be turned into schools when plans were being formulated for the establishment of the modern educational system.[57] The Buddhists could offer little resistance to this program, though they did protest. Just at the close of the monarchical régime there was a mild Buddhist revival that expressed itself in the formation of numerous societies and the publication of a number of periodicals. With the establishment of the Republic the revival quickly passed away. This was in part due to the fact that, "Although the constitution has promised religious liberty and equality of treatment of all religions, yet the government has seen fit to exercise stringent supervision over Buddhism."[58] Buddhist temples and monasteries in large numbers throughout the country have been turned into public buildings. In many of them one finds troops quartered and in many more modern schools are being conducted. The renewed Buddhist revival, under the monk T'ai Hsü, that arose about 1915 has to the present accomplished little. "As yet this spiritual revival in Buddhism is confined to a small group of educated monks and lay brothers. The vast mass of Buddhist monks and nuns (estimated at 400,000 monks and 10,000 nuns) are [sic] untouched by it."[59]

It has already been noted that in connection with the establishment of the new educational system the Manchu régime had decided to make Confucianism the state religion, in the same way that Japan had adopted Shintoism.[60] However, the abolition of the literary examinations in 1905 and the increasing tendency to eliminate the classics as the basis of the educational curricula caused much uneasiness among the conservatives. During the first year or so of the Republic, when the iconoclastic Republicans for the first time gained control of the government, little reverence was shown for Confucianism. Many religious temples were turned into schools and not all Confucian temples escaped this secularization process.[61] At the National Educational Conference held in the summer of 1912, the Minister of Education, Ts'ai Yüan p'ei, proposed to abolish in the schools the special ceremonies held in honor of Confucius. The reasons were, in the first place, Confucianism was not a revealed religion, but a cult and a form of superstition; and secondly, that to impose the cult of Confucianism on the schools would be to violate the religious liberty clause of the Constitution.[62] What Minister Ts'ai would substitute for Confucianism as the unifying element of the nation was, as has been noted above in connection with the educational aims and curricula set forth at this time under his authority, a form of modern nationalism.[63]

However, the wishes of the Republicans, among whom Ts'ai was a leader, were not to be realized at this time. Under the Presidency of Yüan Shih-k'ai there ensued a marked revival of Confucianism in the educational system. In November of 1913, Yüan revealed his attitude toward the doctrine of Confucius when he said it ". . . will be the model to men of all generations and is ever new across a thousand centuries. . . . Now that the new State is founded, it should venerate Confucius more than ever."[64] By a Presidential mandate of February 7, 1914, an attempt was made to establish the Confucian cult as the State religion.[65] Military cults were also revived under Yüan for the purpose of arousing the military spirit among the people (*Shang Wu*). He ordered, November 20, 1914, the special state-worship of two military heroes, *Kuan Yü* and *Yüeh Fei* and twenty-four lesser heroes associated with them.[66] In May, 1915, officers of the Ministry of War swore fidelity to the State before the newly constructed temple of *Yüeh Fei* and *Kuan Yü,* a prince's mansion having been made over for the purpose. In the fall of the same year another ceremony was held there in honor of twenty-four model officers who had been canonized the previous year.[67] The temple of Heaven and the Confucian temple were also refurbished at this time. Yüan actually performed the ceremony at the Altar of Heaven himself.

Following Yüan Shih-k'ai's death, in 1916, Li Yüan-hung became President. The question of rewriting the Constitution was in order. A long and close fight occurred on the question of religious liberty or the establishment of Confucianism as an official sect. Article XI of the new Constitution read, "The Citizens of the Chinese Republic have the liberty, either of honoring Confucius, or of following another religious belief, within the limits of the laws."[68] While Hsü Shih-ch'ang was President a law was passed (1918) authorizing September 4th, Confucius' birthday, as a national holiday on which occasion the national flag was to be everywhere displayed.[69] At present Confucianism has been practically eliminated from the modern educational system and modern nationalism has taken its place. Confucius' birthday has become a nationalist holiday.

Christianity established itself in China during the nineteenth century under the aegis of treaties wrested from the Manchu Government. This was necessary as the Confucian system, as such, was opposed to all sects. This opposition had found expression in the Manchu code, the *Ta Ch'ing Lü Li*.[70] In the treaties religious toleration was secured and the rights of propagation of the faith, of travel, of residence, etc., were guaranteed. This has caused constant opposition to Christianity on the part of the government, the officials, and the literati in general, as well as among the masses who were jealous and resentful of their neighbors who, by becoming Christians, had secured foreign aid in obtaining justice in the courts, or had been exempt from certain taxes. However, the opposition of the Chinese to the rapidly growing system of Christian education in the country became effective only with the rise of the modern nationalist movement. It was through the successful denunciation of nationalist groups that the use of Christian schools to propagate Christianity was effectively curbed and the substitution therefor of the nationalist cult as described above.

The expressed opposition of certain Chinese leaders to the Christian system of education, as controlled by foreigners prior to the establishment of the national system, has already been noted.[71] Throughout the period from 1903, when the modern system of education was established, until 1918, when the mission schools commenced to register with the government, the policy of the government was lax, though tending more and more to bring pressure on them to register. In 1907, for example, the National Board of Education decided that no schools established by foreigners would be registered, but recognition would not be given their graduates for fear of encouraging the extension of foreign-controlled schools and thus hinder the abolition of extraterritoriality.[72] By 1913, however, regulations governing registration were being issued by the Ministry.[73] These regulations were not strictly enforced partly because of the support given to missionaries by their respective governments, and partly due to lack of general opposition within the country, and also, in part, due to the reliance of government schools upon the mission schools for teachers.[74] In 1917 further regulations governing registration of mission schools were promulgated which included the rules that no religious teaching or ceremony should be compulsory and non-Christian students should be admitted to the schools and accorded equal treatment.[75]

Effective opposition to Christian schools developed after 1920. In that year the Young China Association was formed in Peking. Its membership was limited to those without religious faith. The traditional agnosticism and scepticism of the Chinese intellectuals was revived under the stimulus of contact with western philosophies and science. The presence of Bertrand Russell in Peking, where in a course of lectures he attacked Christianity, helped to bring the movement to a head. The first serious outbreak came in 1922 during the convention of the World's Student Christian Federation held in the capital. Prior to the convention, a group of Shanghai students formed an Anti-Christian Federation in direct opposition to it. The opposition centered around two points first, that religion is only a superstition; and second, and more important, that the Christian religion is an expression of imperialism. This was followed in Peking by the organization of the Anti-Religious Federation by groups of students connected with educational institutions in that city.

They declared that all religion had been ruled out by science.[76]

However, these organizations were of little immediate effect and served only to indicate the general drift of the period. The real movement, called the "Restore the Educational Prerogatives Movement," emerged in 1924.[77] Important officials and educators were now at the back of it. A number of factors combined to bring forth active and effective official opposition to Christian education. One of these was the publication of the Burton report of the China Educational Commission in 1922. This report clearly revealed that " . . . the Christian schools constitute a system."[78] Chinese educators viewed this rival system with jealousy and alarm. It should also be stated here, as a contributing factor, that it was a time when the foreign governments were discussing ways of using returned Boxer indemnity funds, and some fear arose among the Chinese that they might give a portion of the funds to mission schools. Not only did this uncontrolled foreign system invade their educational prerogatives, but it was also felt to be denationalizing the students.[79] This conviction was universally held and repeatedly expressed from this time forth.

The movement broke out in the summer of 1924. At the fifth annual conference of the Young China Association, held in July, the following resolution was passed: "That we strongly oppose Christian education which destroys the national spirit of our people and carries on a cultural program in order to undermine Chinese civilization."[80] That same month the National Association for the Advancement of Education at its annual conference held in Nanking requested the government to insist upon the registration of all foreign schools and colleges and to bar all religious instruction.[81]

At this conference the delegates from the three north-eastern provinces (Manchuria) pointed out the cultural exploitation undertaken by Japanese schools in that area. At some of the Japanese schools for Chinese, no Chinese subjects were offered. Furthermore, the Chinese students were required to bow before a picture of the Emperor of Japan. The question of ". . . foreign-controlled schools in China was reviewed and discussed with much heat."[82]

At the national conference of Students' Unions held in August of that year (1924) the "Restore the Educational Prerogatives Movement" was organized. *Pari passu* the Anti-Christian Federation was revived. A mass of literature arose opposing Christianity and mission schools:

> Christianity was condemned on the ground that it was the forerunner of imperialistic exploitation and was accompanied by demands for indemnities and territorial concessions; that it was allied with capitalism; that it destroyed the national spirit of the Chinese; that it had always existed for the strong and depended upon oppression; that converts were attracted by material rewards; that Christians made use of prominent men and flattered the rich; that they were hypocrites; that they meddled in law suits and protected criminals; that Christian schools restrained freedom of thought and action, compelled attendance at worship, hindered the full development of individuals, suppressed patriotism, and were hopelessly conservative and old-fashioned; that Christian ethics and doctrines were untenable; and that Jesus himself was not perfect and was not particularly important.[83]

Further criticisms of Christianity held that it was too peaceful proclaiming a doctrine of peace which was weakening to China. In other words it hindered the development of a nationalistic state.[84]

The National Federation of Provincial Educational Associations at its tenth annual meeting held in Kaifeng in October of 1924 passed a resolution to prevent foreigners from conducting education within the country, unless under the strict control of the Ministry of Education and in conformity and harmony with governmental aims and curricula. The schools were not to propagate religion and there should be no compulsory attendance upon religious courses or ceremonies. Four reasons were stated for all this: first, foreign-controlled schools invaded the educational prerogatives of the nation; second, the type of education given by foreigners was unsuited to Chinese conditions and needs; third, their schools denationalized the students; fourth, the curricula were arranged according to foreign standards and were unsuited to Chinese students.[85]

The Chinese government commenced to promulgate rules governing the registration of mission schools which became more and more severe. The May and June incidents of 1925 which inflamed Chinese nationalism to fever heat greatly stimulated the whole movement. On November 16, 1925 the Ministry of Education of the Peking government promulgated regulations which insisted that all private schools have a Chinese President or Vice-President, that more than half the Board of Directors be Chinese, that religious propaganda should not be conducted, that the curricula conform to those of the Ministry of Education and that attendance upon religious courses be not compulsory.[86] All subsequent rules for registration had this same requirement—that the schools established by foreigners must be controlled by Chinese. This would insure the coöperation of the Chinese Christian staff who naturally coveted the places of power in mission activities. The northern government on November 19, 1927 issued a new set of regulations so drastic that all registered schools ". . . had to exclude all religious teaching and worship from the school curriculum and program" and conform to standards set by the Ministry of Education. The regulations issued by the Nanking government on February 6, 1928 were equally severe.[87]

Following the Tsinan incident in May 1928, when Japanese troops clashed with the Nationalists' forces at that city in Shantung, there was a renewal of the agitation for military education in all schools and at the National Educational Conference held in August of that year it was recommended that military training be included along with physical education in the curricula of middle schools and colleges. In March 1929, the Minister of Education issued regulations for compulsory military training in senior middle schools and colleges. Thus Christian schools which had registered with the government would be forced to provide military training.[88]

The Chinese nationalist movement has now practically triumphed in its struggle against a foreign-controlled system of education within its nation. As time goes on, the number of schools controlled by foreigners will be reduced to a trifling minimum, and meanwhile all privately established schools are being forced to adopt the curricula, aims and textbooks formulated and approved by the Ministry of Education. Nationalistic China, like national states everywhere, is highly intolerant of a type of education or a type of personality that may in any way be branded as unpatriotic or denationalized. Many Christian educators, Chinese and foreigners alike, expressed a willingness to educate for the nationalistic type, as they saw no inconsistency between that type and the "real" Christian. But the Nationalists would not permit them this privilege. They would not permit them to use the school as a means for propagating their religious faith.[89] Religious toleration was not to be extended to this domain. The Chinese "state" cherishes unto itself the educational system as the most effective tool in propagating its own religion—Nationalism—and is highly intolerant of any other religious group usurping that power. Nationalism is still flushed with its first victories in China and may, therefore, be at the height of its intolerance. However, the future is uncertain and renewed waves of nationalistic sentiment may extend the present period of fanatical intolerance indefinitely. On the other hand, the old traditional easy-going psychology of the Chinese may reassert itself. That will largely depend, as usually in the past, upon the treatment accorded the nation by Japan and the western nations. The Chinese government may come in time to tolerate really Christian schools, but of course never in any significant number. If the government can succeed in carrying out to the letter its present regulations with regard to privately established schools it is apparent that there will no longer be "Christian" schools, in any fundamental sense of the word, in China.

SUMMARY AND CONCLUSIONS

Modern education was forced upon China by the aggressive impact of the West. It was resorted to in the beginning as a means of strengthening the nation along military and naval lines. Thus at first only that type of western education which would build up a modern army and navy was introduced. It was only after the humiliating defeat suffered at the hands of Japan in 1894-95 the idea spread that in order to have a strong nation along military lines the economic and industrial resources of the nation must be developed, which in turn meant educating all the people. Out of this enlarged view grew the first modern system of education, However, the first aim of creating a modern army and navy has remained a dominant and motivating factor to the present.

From the outset the spirit of modern militarism was introduced into the developing educational system. This idea of a "nation in arms" was a new one for China and came directly from the West and Japan. It has continued to spread and has now become deeply entrenched in the educational system.

Throughout the period from 1895 to 1930 the field of education was more or less assumed, and in recent years openly asserted, to be the prerogative of the state, to be used by it as a tool to enhance its power and prestige. This attitude is well founded on long established tradition dating back to the second century before Christ when Han emperors and officials built up orthodox Confucianism to become a psychological foundation for the newly formed Empire and a barrier against the feudalistic traditions of earlier centuries. Under this conception, reinforced by the dogmatic spirit of modern nationalism, education by all private groups is now rigidly controlled and forced into harmony with the spirit and aims of the state system. The nationalists have successfully eliminated the competing religions of Buddhism, Christianity and Confucianism, and are preventing the believers of these religions from using schools as a means for propagandizing their faiths.

The first system of education adopted was modelled directly upon that of Japan as being nearest in harmony with the spirit and aims of an autocratic monarchy. After 1919 the American system of education was consciously adopted being more in spirit with the aims of a democratic republic.

However, under all the systems of education adopted from 1903 on, the spirit of modern nationalism continued to develop and spread. Curricula and textbooks were so designed as to awaken among the students a self-conscious awareness of what was called their peculiar national characteristics, of the dangers threatening the existence of the nation and of their supreme duty in life to be loyal, even unto death, to the nation. In view of these aims it is not surprising to find that over 95 per cent of the students in China leave school knowing nothing of the world at large save as it has unhappily trampled upon China's sovereign rights.

In order to arouse this spirit of nationalism among the students the curricula and textbooks have been consciously controlled by the educators. Not only has a fair treatment of the world at large, its history and its contributions been consciously eliminated in favor of the nationalistic emphasis, but also material designed to fit the student to his more vital life in the family and community has been reduced to a minimum, so that the conception of the nation as the supreme form of social grouping may be indoctrinated and all vital problems be seen as national ones which the state alone can solve through its political machinery. The conscious way in which this was done is of the utmost significance. It is not a natural inherent development, but an artificial one.

There was one period of exception to this general development which occurred between 1919 and 1925. It was the period of greatest breakdown of central authority in China and accompanying it was a development of the federalistic idea of local autonomy in all matters political as well as educational. At this time some of the better American textbooks on civics were adopted and used in the schools. In them the nation was seen as only one of many social groupings, commencing with the family and culminating in the world community. A considerable amount of space was devoted to local problems and needs, as well as to international problems. But new waves of nationalistic fervor swept the country after 1925 and crushed this spirit of liberalism and substituted for it a form of dogmatic fanatical nationalism that has since found its way into all curricula and textbooks.

Confucianism was finally disestablished as the state "religion" after 1916. By 1925 Confucianistic teachings had been reduced to a trifling minimum in the modern textbooks in widest use. Modern educators believe that nationalism is a more effective means for arousing supreme loyalty to the state than "old-fashioned" Confucianism with its more balanced emphasis upon the "five relationships" of life.

The adoption of the outward forms, the modes of expression and the philosophy of modern nationalism was a highly conscious, artificial process. Japan and the West were frequent models imitated in this development. The selection of creeds, symbols, and ceremonial forms such as flags and songs were likewise consciously adopted.

Though the spirit of modern nationalism has thoroughly permeated the educational system, it is still largely confined to intellectual circles. It has found a certain amount of expression among the commercial classes, a lesser degree among the laboring classes and scarcely at all among the farmers. Its greatest failure to date has been its inability to convert the numerous armies in China and their leaders to its "gospel." The fruits of militarism in China, a militarism which was consciously adopted and is still fostered to strengthen the nation, have only served to weaken it, and to bring untold suffering upon millions of peaceful people.

Modern nationalistic education in China is still far from achieving the goal of a unified, centralized sovereign Republic envisaged by Chinese leaders responsible for its adoption and promotion. While in the realm of the country's relations with the other nations there exists a common aim held by all factions, there is striking lack of harmony as to internal policy. Whether this modern educational system, when universally extended throughout the land, can effectively spread the spirit of nationalism to the extent necessary to overcome the well-nigh insuperable barriers of sectionalism remains for the future to determine.

APPENDIX I

A Digest of Textbooks Used in the Mass Education Movement and the Most Popular Textbooks Used in the Primary and Middle Schools of China from 1905 to 1929

The order of treatment is as follows: Mass Education texts; Historical texts; texts on Ethics, Civics, Citizenship, San Min Chu I; Readers and Geography. Within each category the texts are chronologically arranged. The average size of an edition for the mass education texts, as well as for lower and upper primary texts is a minimum of 5,000. For middle-school texts the minimum is 3,000-5,000. These figures apply to the Commercial Press texts and were supplied by the Editor-in-Chief. The Chung Hwa Press editions the author judges to be about the same size.

I. CHU, CHING-NÊNG AND T'AO, CHIH-HSING, *P'ing Min Ch'ien Tzŭ K'ê* ("The People's One Thousand Character Lessons"). 4 vols., Shanghai: Commercial Press, 1st ed., Aug., 1923. Vol. I reached 162d ed. in Oct., 1926; vol. IV reached only 115th ed. in Aug., 1927. The preface states that the book has three aims:

1. To cultivate man's nature and promote the spirit of coöperation necessary in a Republican country.

2. To train the students to write letters, keep accounts and to compose useful literary articles.

3. To teach them to read books and newspapers and thereby give them the very fundamentals of a superior education.

In volume 2, page 16 the national song is printed. Volume 3 has several songs about the flag and country, while volume 4 contains biographies of Christ, Sun Yat-sen and Yüan Shih-k'ai.

This set was the first printed for the mass education movement, apart from the one printed by James Yen (No. II below) while he was working with the Y.M.C.A. It is confused and vague. It fails to present the conception of citizenship which the later one emphasizes. This set prints a picture of the five-barred flag adopted after the Revolution, while the later one reproduces the Kuomintang flag.

II. YEN, JAMES, AND FU, D. C., *P'ing Min Ch'ien Tzŭ K'ê* ("The Foundation Characters"). 4 vols. Shanghai: National Committee Y.M.C.A. of China, 1st ed., Feb., 1922; 14th rev. ed., April, 1928. (5 cents a copy.)

This is the first set put out by James Yen and is much less mature than those that follow. It has only seven lessons of a nationalistic character.

III. SHIH MIN CH'IEN TZŬ K'ê ("Towns' People Thousand Character Lessons"). 4 vols., Shanghai: Commercial Press, 1st ed., Aug., 1927. Prepared by National Association Mass Education Movement. (7 cents each.)

The preface states that over 3,000,000 copies of the old series (No. I above) were printed and sold. This makes approximately 800,000 sets. This present revised edition is based upon the 1,300 most frequent characters, found by a committee, in 1,000,000 characters of printed matter. The characters selected were further scrutinized and criticized by many outstanding scholars.

The aims as set forth in the first volume are:

1. To enable the people to read material relating to everyday life in the towns of China.

2. To give the common people a general education in citizenship which the leaders in the Movement believe to be the basis of all education. Mr. Ch'ên Chu-shan, who is in charge of the department of education for citizenship in the Movement in-

formed the author that it is the social rather than the legal concept of citizenship which he wishes to emphasize—teaching
the people to coöperate in solving their own local problems.
He views the political sphere as only one of many.

The ninety-six lessons in the four volumes are to be covered in four months. The material is selected and arranged in
the most approved fashion of modern pedagogy. Practically
all of the ninety-six lessons are illustrated.

Volume I

Lesson 20. The Citizen. "The citizen is an upright man."
Citizens love to serve their country. Their duty is to serve their
country first and later attend to their private affairs. They
fight for public rights and not alone for private ends. (The
picture illustrating this lesson is that of a Chinese man and
woman bending under the weight of the world on which a map
of China is outlined and in the background is a crowd of people both young and old rushing forward to help them.)

Lesson 22. This lesson is an explanation of the "Double-Ten
Anniversary"—October 10th, the Chinese Independence Day. It
is illustrated by a picture with many people carrying flags.

Lesson 23. "The Chinese people should use Chinese goods.
If they do not do so it will be difficult to find a market for
Chinese goods. Chinese goods ought to improve in quality. If
they are not improved it will be difficult to get men to use
them."

Lesson 24. This lesson on Patriotism extols the beauties of
the country; the size and strength of the population; its ancient
origins; the Republic and the principle of equality.

Volume II

Lesson 1. The Masses are here asserted to be the basis of
the nation. They must be revived that the nation may be saved
and the peace of the world promoted.

Lesson 18. Chinese commercial guilds are considered in this
lesson. The old guilds, it states, were good, but now that there

is economic competition with other countries they must organize modern chambers of commerce, as a means of defense against foreign economic aggression.

Lesson 23. China's national shame and lost sovereignty is illustrated by a Chinese stripped to the waist and tied to a post while sitting on a map of China.

Volume III

Lessons 11-12. These lessons deal with Chinese products and resources.

Lesson 14. The necessity of organizing themselves against foreign economic aggression is urged upon the industrialists and merchants.

Lesson 17. On Mutual Love. There are portraits of Confucius, Moti, and Jesus with their sayings on mutual love.

Lessons 21-24. Chinese Geography is considered in these lessons which teach that the foundation of patriotism is coöperation. "Four hundred million with the heart of one, will have strength to build a new China." "Chinese emigrants are many and widely scattered."

Volume IV

Lesson 7. Although 8,000,000 emigrants are away from home, they still love the fatherland and promote Chinese education and have organized themselves into societies to protect one another.

Lesson 9. The Nation is here conceived of as an organization of a people with sovereign rights. These rights come from the people and are exercised by the people.

Lesson 10. This is a lesson on government. If the government is good the people are united; if bad, they can overthrow it.

Lesson 12. An outline of Chinese history is given, commencing with Huang-ti, the mythical founder of the Chinese race.

By way of summary fifteen lessons are devoted to the subject of national affairs. Twelve of these are purely nationalistic in tone. This comprises one-eighth of the material presented.

This series was printed before the Kuomintang successes and hence has nothing on the San Min Chu I.

IV. *Kai Chêng Nêng Min Ch'ien Tzŭ K'ê* (Revised edition "Farmers' Thousand Character Lessons"). 4 vols. Shanghai: Commercial Press, 1st ed., June, 1928. Prepared by the National Association Mass Education Movement.

Volume I

There are lessons in the first volume on the necessity of going to school to learn to read so that one may become a good citizen and help to make a strong nation.

Volume II

One lesson is on the Double-Ten Anniversary; there are others on good roads, hygiene, the silk worm, etc.

Volume III

Lesson 15. Sun Yat-sen, the Kuomintang and the San Min Chu I are treated here.

Volume IV

There is nothing in this volume of a nationalistic bent.

This series has only two lessons of a nationalistic nature. The remainder of the material deals with matters and problems of a vital nature to the farmer in his local environment.

V. *Shih Ping Ch'ien Tzŭ K'ê* ("The Soldiers' Thousand Character Lessons"). 4 vols., Peking: Mass Education Movement, Jan. 1, 1928.

Volume I

This volume is practically the same as the series for the Towns' People.

Volume II

Lesson 9. Soldiers are admonished to pay people for food and other commodities which they buy and not cause undue suffering.

Lesson 18. If there is peace within the country commerce will develop, the people will prosper and the nation become strong. The army should protect the common people. Two other lessons emphasize this same conception.

Volume III

Lesson 4. This lesson is on Yüeh Fei, China's great general and irredentist, patron saint of the militarists.

Lesson 6. On Sun Yat-sen and the San Min Chu I—The Three Principles of the People.

Lesson 15. On Loving the People. It resurrects and discusses the old Chinese officials and generals who were renowned for their devotion to the public welfare.

Lesson 20. The story of Hua Man-lien, a famous woman warrior of old China is here told.

There are also three lessons on Chinese geography in this volume.

Volume four was not examined.

VI. *Ch'ien Tzŭ K'ê Hsiu Shên Yung Pên.* ("Textbook of One Thousand Characters for Self-Instruction") 4 vols., Shanghai: Commercial Press, Vol. I first published Aug., 1927, Vols. III and IV published Mar., 1928, by Mass Education Movement.

This series was designed to be used by students who have taken any one of the foregoing series.

Volume III

Lesson 2. The Clan. Love is the most beautiful of all virtues. There should be mutual love not only in the family and the clan, but it should extend to friends, the village people, all the country and finally to all mankind. Thus will man's shortcomings be diminished.

Lesson 5. The farmer is the basis of the nation. Because China's methods of production are poor and the country disturbed, foreign goods penetrate everywhere. Therefore the

Chinese must boycott foreign goods or the foreigners will secure China's wealth.

Lesson 6. Jesus is portrayed as a man of love, who favoured peace and equality. Though he died two thousand years ago his spirit is still with us. He belongs to all the world.

By way of summary, of the Thousand Character Lessons published by the Mass Education Movement it may be stated that they are not as strongly biased and nationalistic as the texts reviewed below. They were written in the spirit and from the viewpoint prevailing among educators in the 1920-1924 period when coöperation and citizenship were the dominant ideals. Citizenship is seen as active and responsible participation in group affairs whether of local, village, provincial, national or even international nature. The rise of the Kuomintang to power on the wave of nationalism that swept the country after May, 1925 has induced some change in that one or two lessons in the later series where mention is made of the San Min Chu I. Whether or not they will be forced to introduce more of that party's tactics and philosophy remains to be seen. However, it may be said that the books are prevailingly nationalist in tone, though negatively so. The only conception of the foreigner set forth is that of the aggressive merchant in the port cities.

HISTORY TEXTBOOKS

VII. *Chinese History for Beginners:* New Middle School Textbooks Series. Shanghai: Chung Hwa Press, 1st ed. Aug., 1923; 7th ed. Aug., 1925.

This is an old-fashioned history made up largely of military and political events. There are only a few pages, at the close of the book, on the literary revolution in China, and on the social and economic conditions of the nation. It is nationalistic in tendency.

VIII. *Chinese History of different Dynasties for Middle Schools.* (Rev. ed.) 2 vols. Shanghai: Commercial Press, 1st ed., 1910; 11th ed., 1916. (Only Vol. 2 seen.)

Only one-sixth is devoted to the history of the last one hundred years. The above work (No. VII), which is a much later one, devoted over one-fourth of its space to the same period. It treats the subject more dispassionately than No. VII, but it is largely a military and political history. No social, cultural or economic phases are presented.

IX. Ku, Chieh-kang, and Wang, Chung-ch'i, *Hsien Tai Ch'u Chung Chiao K'ê Shu, Pên Kuo Shih*. ("Chinese History for Use in Lower Middle Schools.") 3 vols. Shanghai: Commercial Press; 1st ed., Sept., 1923; 3d ed., May, 1924.

This set was edited by Hu Shih. The preface states that history should concern itself with real affairs and not confine itself to mere dynastic annals. The work commences with a long introduction on the geographical and racial basis of Chinese civilization. It adopts a critical attitude and presents various theories of the origins of the races of Eastern Asia. It continues by describing the seven races of China, including the Miaotze and the Koreans, reaching the conclusion that the Chinese "race" is only a collective name and not a pure ethnographic group. Speaking of Korea the book states that although the Koreans are now subject to Japan they look to China to rescue them and preserve their culture. This work, written by two leaders in China's modern schools of historical criticism omits the model emperors Yao and Shun and the lore connected with them. The result was it failed to gain the approval of the Board of Education and when the Nationalists came into power the book was banned and the Commercial Press fined a million dollars, it is rumored by the Shanghai Kuomintang headquarters!

X. Wang, En-chüeh, *Hsin Shih Tai Shih Chieh Shih Chiao K'ê Shu* ("Modern Age World History Textbook"). 2 vols. Shanghai: Commercial Press, 5th ed., 1927. Published under the auspices of the Modern Age Educational Society.

This set is for use in the middle schools. The aim, as stated in the introduction, is to trace the rise of each people and not of political entities. Pages one to five give the most advanced and enlightened conception of history found in the West. The work clearly shows the influence of Wells' "Outline of History." It speaks of the sphere of history as being very large and not to be bound to national or even racial history, but enough material must be included to explain origins of all great movements. The work commences with evolutionary origin of the earth and finally of descent of man from anthropoid ape, after which follows the rise of civilized society in the Nile and Euphrates valleys. One of the diagrams is apparently taken from Wells' book.

XI. Chou, Fu-ju, *Hsin Chuan Ch'u Chi Chung Hsüeh Chiao K'ê Shu, Shih Chieh Shih* ("World History"). 2 vols. Shanghai: Commercial Press, February, 1925.

Only the first volume of this work has been seen by the author. The set is for use in the lower middle schools. The objects of the work as set forth in the introduction are as follows:

1. To study conditions bringing about changes and developments in the life of mankind.

2. To show that man's psychology is everywhere the same in order to create in the student the spirit of love and mutual help.

3. To guide the students and to arouse in them a desire to read history.

This work is much the same as the one described above, having the same illustrations, the same division of material and manner of treatment.

XII. Wang, Chung-ch'i and Hu Shih, *Hsin Shih Tai Pên Kuo Shih Chiao K'ê Shu* ("New Age Chinese History"). 2 vols. Shanghai: Commercial Press, Sept., 1927.

This history like the above mentioned (No. IX) abolished the old system of dating and dissolved the myths clustering about the traditional account of the origins and early history of the Chinese people. In the introduction the authors pointed out the two viewpoints from which they aimed to use the materials of history. First, in the older periods, to emphasize the arts, the thought and the customs, tracing their origin and development. Then, in the modern period, to emphasize imperialism and the development of democracy.

XIII. Fu Lin, *Hsin Shih Tai Li Shih Chiao K'ê Shu* ("The New Age History"). 4 vols. Shanghai: Commercial Press, 1927.

This little history for higher primary students had the approval of the University Council (Ta Hsüeh Yüan). Though the title might imply that it dealt with universal, or world history, in reality only Chinese history is presented. No other history is required in the primary schools of China today. This set had a very large sale. The first volume reached its 65th edition within fifteen months after it was first published; the second volume its 60th edition in seventeen months; and the third volume its 45th edition in eleven months. The fourth volume was not examined by the author. Approximately 800,000 copies were sold to four hundred thousand students in one year. (As the Commercial Press supplies about 60 per cent of the textbooks in China it can be safely deduced that there were over 600,000 students in the higher primary schools during 1928.)

The first volume begins with the traditional mythological account of the origin of the Chinese people recounting the unique and glorious history of Huang-ti, Fu-hsi, Yao and Shun, etc. By the middle of the second volume the whole history of China to the Anglo-Chinese war of 1840 is presented! The usual interpretation of the "Opium" war is given and then, after recounting indignities suffered by China at the hands of the imperialistic powers, it hastens on to record the history of the Revolution in its political aspects, including a biography of Sun Yat-sen. In volume three the development of the Kuomintang is set forth as well as the history of the Republic and of democratic government in general.

TEXTS ON ETHICS, MORALITY AND THE SAN MIN CHU I

XIV. *Tsui Hsien Ch'u Têng Hsiao Hsüeh Hsiu Shên Chiao K'ê Shu* ("Ethical culture text for lower primary schools"). 10 vols. Shanghai: Commercial Press, 1905.

The preface states, "It is constantly said that moral culture, mental culture and physical culture constitute true education. This is true, but moral culture is the root of all; on this, ancient and modern, Chinese and foreigners are all agreed.

"The Chinese books which teach morals are numberless, but abstract discussion of principle and abstruse applications are unsuited to infantile minds. This series selects the wise sayings of the ancients and their grave acts and sets these forth [with illustrative pictures] as examples for the children of today." (Quoted from Darroch, John, "Chinese Textbooks," *Journal of the North China Branch of the Royal Asiatic Society*, Vol. XXXVII [1906], 208-209).

Neighborliness, charity, self-control and duties in the home are the chief subjects dealt with. All are written in Mandarin. This work marks the first break with the traditional methods of teaching the classics by rote. Under the influence of western pedagogical methods as introduced by the missionary textbooks, this series selects the material and grades it to suit the minds of the children.

XV. *Republican Ethical Readers for Higher Primary Schools*. 5 vols. Shanghai: Commercial Press, 1912.

This series written just after the establishment of the Republic uses the classical *wen li*. For the most part the lessons are vague and indefinite in reference and in content.

XVI. *Republican Ethical Readers for Higher Primary Schools*. 6 vols. Shanghai: Commercial Press, 1912.

With this series Chinese educators commence to substitute for vague, general principles of morality centering about the home, or the traditional five relationships of Chinese society, incarnated in heroes of old, concrete deeds of a contemporaneous political nature with a view to making the child nationally conscious. The result is we find lessons on the recent revolution, several lessons on the bravery of soldiers, on loyalty to the country, and one on liberty.

XVII. FAN, PING-CH'ING, *Kung Ho Kuo Chiao K'ê Shu-Hsiu Shên Yao I* ("Republican Series: Essentials of Ethics for Middle Schools"). 2 vols. Shanghai: Commercial Press, 1913; 26th rev. ed., Mar., 1922.

This series, which reached its 26th edition by 1922, was written in close coöperation with the newly reorganized—as a result of the 1911 revolution—Ministry of Education, and received its approval. The fourth chapter of volume two stresses the student's duty to his family or clan. It points out that the family is the foundation of a national society and that the nation is the natural and supreme form of social grouping. The fifth chapter has a section on "Our Country's Peculiar Characteristics," stating that China has a different source of ethics than the West. In China government is based on morals and in the West on law. The book continues by discussing the traditional five relationships of society and states that the first of those relationships, which was formerly concerned with the loyalty of the subject to the Emperor, should now be changed to loyalty toward the nation.

The series constantly compares Chinese and western morals and religions, evidently seeking a synthesis, but ending up by emphasizing the value of Confucianism and the classics. It admonishes the students not to give up the classics; if there is no time to read them all in the schools, they should continue to read them upon leaving school.

It is clearly evident in this series that the half-way stage between the traditional teaching of the Confucian classics by rote, and the inculcation of the conception of the nationalistic citizen in the civics readers described below where the old Confucian morality is completely abandoned, has been reached.

XVIII. Li, Pu-ch'ing, *Hsin Chih Hsiu Shên Chiao Pên* ("The New System Ethical Culture Texts"). 4 vols. Shanghai: Chung Hwa Press, 1914.

This series received the personal supervision of Fan Yüan-lien, sometime Minister of Education, and secured the approval of the Ministry of Education. It obtained a wide sale reaching its twenty-fourth edition in 1922. This set together with set No. XVII supplied fully 90 per cent of the demand for ethical culture readers in the middle schools for the period 1914 to 1922. The first volume treats of the individual and his place in the world. The national viewpoint is constantly presented—"nation" and "world" being practically synonymous terms. There are frequent quotations from Confucius and Mencius. On page forty-four we find a plea for the necessity of militarizing the nation and training soldiers. The following page emphasizes the necessity of fighting against the influx of foreign goods. In the second volume society and the nation are made one. It discusses public rights, liberty, equality, education, and the importance of these to a nation in this modern world of warring nationalities. In patriotic sentiment man's personality finds a high form of expression. The third volume emphasizes the students' responsibility toward themselves, their race, mankind, and all living things. The fourth stresses China's special characteristics. It emphasizes the uniqueness and implied superiority of Chinese civilization.*

* For a translation and analysis of the eleven most widely used texts on *Hsiu Shen* in the primary, middle, and normal schools for girls as well as boys in 1920, see: Wieger, Père Léon, "Moralisme official des écoles, en 1920," *Chine Moderne*. Vol. I, Hsien Hsien, 1921.

The following references relate to material designed to arouse the students' national patriotism: For lessons on the State, see pp. 211, 213, 245, 324, 371, 397, 402, 460; on Patriotism, pp. 104, 170, 180, 194, 203, 241, 293, 330, 345, 350, 403, 460, 461 (This subject has the second largest number of pages devoted to it of all the subjects treated in the series) ; Xenophobie (Chauvinism), pp. 206, 331,

XIX. Shêng, Tsai-hsiang, *Shang Yeh Tao Tê* ("Business Ethics"). Shanghai: Commercial Press, 1915; 6th ed., 1920.

This text was granted approval by the Ministry of Education for use in the newly established commercial schools. This is something new for China, it states in the preface, though Europe and Japan have such schools now. A section on patriotism urges the merchants to coöperate against foreign economic aggression. Some 20-30,000 copies were sold in five years.

XX. Yüan, Fang-chün, *Hsin Shih Hsiu Shên Chiao K'ê Shu* ("Chinese Ethical Readers"). 8 vols. Shanghai: Chung Hwa Press, 1916; 64th ed., 1923.

A little series for primary schools which was written under the supervision of Fan Yüan-lien and obtained the approval of the Ministry of Education. Some 350,000 copies were sold by 1923. It is the companion set to number XVIII above. The first and second volumes contain nothing but pictures. The set shows strong Japanese influence, Fan having previously studied in Japan. Volume four has a lesson on soldiers. The text beginning with this volume is in the easiest possible *wen li,* or classical style. The scenes and stories in the whole set are drawn for the most part from old Chinese life. In volume six some of the subjects treated are Yüeh Fei, one of China's greatest generals and an irredentist; wars and the nation; a nation and its people; the Red Cross; Washington; Lincoln; family virtues and public virtues. The last volume emphasizes national patriotism, the value and need of soldiers for China, and of education to make the nation strong. The general tone and temper of the set is strongly militaristic and nationalistic.

403, 430, 460, 461; Duties to state, pp. 74, 154, 244, 264, 440, 441, 445, 463.

In all about sixty out of 464 pages are devoted to material aiming directly to arouse the spirit of nationalism.

XXI. Wêng, Chang-chung, *Kung Min Mo Fan* ("The Model Citizen"). Shanghai: Chung Hwa Press, 1914.

Though not a text, this book is introduced here because it was perhaps the earliest treatment of the conceptions and nature of modern citizenship in the Chinese language. It has had a wide sale reaching its sixth edition in 1926. It was, no doubt, influential in preparing the way for the civics readers, discussed below, which were ultimately to displace ethical readers, reviewed above. This change commenced to take place after 1921. In his preface the author states that the ethical readers are inadequate for the new day when the citizen's relation to society is the dominating factor. The old family loyalty and viewpoint must be extended to include the nation and even the whole world. Seeing this need in China the author has selected passages from famous western writers on the subject, translated them and given them forth to help his country in the way of moral education. Many of the translations are drawn from the utterances of outstanding western patriots setting forth their conceptions of the duties and responsibilities of citizenship.

XXII. Chou, Chih-kan, *et al.*, *Kung Min Hsüeh K'ê Ch'êng Ta Kang* ("Outlines of a Course in Civics"). Shanghai: Commercial Press, 1923.

This outline was sponsored by the Chinese Association for the Advancement of Education. The preface states that it was drawn from a study of American civics textbooks and owes its origin to a committee appointed by the Association at its first annual meeting in order to investigate citizenship education.

XXIII. Kao Yang and T'ao, Hui-tsêng, *Hsin Chuan Ch'u Chi Chung Hsüeh Chiao K'ê Shu-Kung Min* ("Up-to-date Series, Civics"). 3 vols. Shanghai: Commercial Press, 1925.

This series follows the outline for the course given out by the sixth annual conference of the National Federation of Educational Associations save that the suggested fourth volume on hygiene is omitted. This set is for junior middle schools. It obtained a wide sale, nearly 70,000 copies being sold within one year. The first volume deals with ethics: individual, family, social, or community, national, and even international. The second volume concerns itself with law and government. The national view predominates. Considerable space, however, is devoted to the village, *hsien* (district), city and provincial organization. The last volume treats of economic problems from a national viewpoint.

This is indeed an "up-to-date" set, the last word in bourgeois, liberal economic, legal and nationalist theories of society and government. For example the section on national morality in volume one (p. 84) commences: "The nation is one form of social organization." This objective attitude, however, is not always maintained.

XXIV. Ku, Shu-lin, and P'an, Wên-an, *Kung Min Hsü Chih* ("What a Citizen Should Know"). Shanghai: Commercial Press, 1923.

A civics reader, for use in the middle schools. About 20,000 copies were sold in two years. The authors point out the difference between the old conservative Confucian morality and the modern, progressive conception. Lincoln, Washington, Franklin, Roosevelt, Kant and many other westerners are quoted. The authors advocate the small family as in the West (p. 47). They agree that China's great weakness is due to the lack of a sense of responsibility on the part of its citizens. They quote the former United States Minister to China, Mr. Schurman, to that effect.

In the discussion on national morality, the authors point to the United States as being a shining example of a nation whose people are motivated by national morality and ruled by laws. No doubt the authors are returned students from America. In order to arouse patriotism the students are led to contrast China with other nations and education should be called on to assist in the process. The highly developed family organization is held to be the reason for the lack of patriotism among the Chinese.

The authors, contend, in their discussion of nationalism and internationalism, that international morality must be developed along national lines as the day of the world community (Ta T'ung) is yet far distant. This is the period of nationalities. Yet the spirit of coöperation between nations should be fostered and the League of Nations strengthened. Before the war international relations were conducted by a few in secret and this was a cause of war. In a real democracy the people should control the conduct of foreign affairs.

XXV. *Up-to-Date Civics.* 4 vols. Shanghai: Commercial Press, 1924.

This series treats of the subject in the same manner as the one reviewed above (No. XXIV), save in simpler language as it is written for higher primary school students. Like the other series, it apparently did not have the approval of the Ministry of Education. Over fifty thousand sets were sold during the first half year.

These two sets of civic readers are as broad and liberal in their treatment of the subject as can be found anywhere. The emphasis is on nationalist ethics, but it is mild in comparison with the extremely nationalistic *San Min Chu I* textbooks which practically displaced these in the schools by 1930.

XXVI. Shu Hsin-ch'êng, *Hsin Chung Hsüeh Chiao K'ê Shu-Ch'u Chi Kung Min K'ê Pên* ("Citizenship"). 3 vols. Shanghai: Chung Hwa Press, 1923; 14th ed., 1928.

This series by the nationalistic Chung Hwa Press is for junior middle school students. It was written by a man who knows something about the history of Chinese education, but apparently knows little about what a civics text should contain. The last volume is made up almost entirely of contemporary, passing events. Great emphasis is placed on extraterritoriality, the concessions, and recent international events. Much nationalistic propaganda is gathered out of all this. Yet the book has the approval of the Ministry of Education whereas the much better Commercial Press texts reviewed above did not secure it. It took five years for this set to reach its fourteenth edition, however.

Another set of civics readers for higher primary students published by the same press is equally inadequate. It appeared in 1923 in four volumes and reached its 28th edition within three years. The material is poorly organized, vague and scattered, treating of everything from the sinking of the "Titanic" to the organization of the Chinese district. Yet it was granted the approval of the Ministry of Education.

XXVII. CHANG, CHIU-JU, *San Min Chu I Chiao Yü Hsüeh* ("Studies in San Min Chu I Education"). Shanghai: Commercial Press, 1928.

A general treatment of the manner of instructing pupils in the Three People's Principles of Sun Yat-sen. At the outset it informs the teacher that Militarism, Communism and Imperialism are the three great enemies of Dr. Sun's principles. Then the author continues by showing the relation of these principles to Socialism, Nationalism, Religion, Internationalism, and Individualism, etc. He quotes Sun to the effect that the Nation must be built on the race and only after that is accomplished will the period of the World Community (*Shih Chieh Ta T'ung*) he ushered in. The author concludes by stating that the San Min Chu I are a real step toward an international society of a socialistic type. Throughout the book western writers are frequently quoted including Plato, Aristotle, Hegel and Fichte. The author has suggestions on how to teach the three principles and stresses the importance of teaching the history of the Kuomintang, or Nationalist party.

XXVIII. LI YANG, *Hsin Shih Tai San Min Chu I Chiao K'ê Shu* ("New Series San Min Chu I Readers"). 4 vols. Shanghai: Commercial Press, 1927-1928.

Written under the supervision of Wong Yün-wu, editor-in-chief of the Commercial Press, this series secured the approval of the University Council (*Ta Hsüeh Yüan*). It had a wide sale, the first volume reaching its 135th edition in a year and a half, and the last volume its 80th edition in seven months! This makes an average of 450,000 copies sold of each volume in the set during 1928. According to the preface this series presents in a form suitable for higher primary students not only the San Min Chu I of Sun Yat-sen, but also his other principle lectures, his *Outlines for the Reconstruction of China*, his *International Development of China*, as well as the resolutions and important pronouncements of the Nationalist party. Each of the first three volumes deals with one of the three principles. The fourth and last volume presents along with a history of the party the other works referred to just above. In the first volume there is a long discussion of foreign imperialism. This discussion vigorously asserts that when China is strong it will help the Burmese, Annamese and Koreans to recover their lost rights. This action will help bring about the world community (*Ta T'ung chih ch'ih*). (See Vol. I, pp. 29, 30.)

XXIX. WANG, YUN-WU, ed., *Hsin Shih Tai, San Min Chu I Chiao Pên* ("New Age San Min Chu I Texts") 3 vols. Shanghai: Commercial Press, 1927-28.

This three volume work for use in the junior middle schools was written under the supervision of the Editor-in-chief of the Commercial Press and received the approval of the University Council. An average of forty editions a year were sold. The material in this set is the same as in the one reviewed above, (No. XXVIII) only more advanced and fuller.

XXX. HU, YÜ-CHIH, *Hsin Shih Tai San Min Chu I Chiao K'ê Shu* ("New Age San Min Chu I Reader"). 3 vols. Shanghai: Commercial Press, 1927.

The first two volumes of this series, which is for use in the junior middle schools, also had the approval of the University Council. Volume one reached its thirtieth edition within one year, and the other two volumes sold equally well. This series differs from the one above in not being as strictly Kuomintang in its makeup. For one thing it has a chapter in the first volume on the World Community (*Shih Chieh Ta T'ung*) (pp. 88-90) which is lacking in all the later series. The third volume did not receive the approval of the University Council as it sponsored communism. The Commercial Press published it, but did not write the text, though it wrote the first two volumes. The set appeared at a crucial time when the communist wing was struggling with the right wing for mastery of Shanghai. Interesting to note, as usual in China since the establishment of the Republic, the political struggles have been directly reflected in the textbooks.

XXXI. CHÊNG CH'ANG, *Hsin Chung Hwa Chiao K'ê Shu-San Min Chu I* ("The Three Principles of the People"). 6 vols. Shanghai: Chung Hwa Press, 1929.

This set, the first two volumes of which have been seen, is for junior middle schools. Volume one (pp. 42-44) has an interesting chapter on the relation of the San Min Chu I to Chinese civilization. A clear attempt is made to tie it up with the past relating it to Mencius and Confucius, as well as to the century old Chinese conceptions of moral conduct (*Tao Tê*). *Tao Tê* according to the author of the set is Humanism and Equality combined. China has in this conception the basis for the World Community.

XXXII. CHU, TZŬ-CH'ÊN, *Hsin Shih Tai San Min Chu I Chiao K'ê Shu,* ("New Age San Min Chu I Readers"). 8 vols. Shanghai: Commercial Press, 1927.

This series of readers for the lower primary school students was approved by the University Council. It had a wide sale, reaching its 205th edition within two years, so approximately 4,000,000 children were supplied with these readers in that time. In the third volume we read of China's many talented inventors and sages. At the outset a picture of Huang-ti, China's mythological emperor, is given. On the second page the student is informed that China invented the compass, and a picture of a modern compass is given. The statement on the next page, that Chinese first invented printing, is accompanied by a picture of a modern printing press. In the case of both inventions the children will be ignorant of the important part played by other peoples in the perfecting of both the compass and the printing press, unless the teacher informs them. Otherwise an excellent opportunity to show the interdependence of mankind is lost. However, in the case of gunpowder while acknowledging that Chinese first discovered it, the text readily gave credit to foreigners for perfecting it as an instrument of destruction. As a matter of fact hand grenades were used as far back as the Yüan dynasty, in the thirteeenth and fourteenth centuries, by Chinese armies. Other lessons tell of the skill of former Chinese in making silk, tea, porcelain and in the construction of bridges. Then there are lessons on three of China's greatest sages: Confucius, Mencius, and Laotze. This is followed by a number of lessons describing the rise of science in the West and listing the mechanical achievements that the foreigners developed on this scientific basis. The conclusion says that if the Chinese are to solve the problem of livelihood for the people they must study science, manufacture their own goods and boycott foreign goods. Only in that way will they become wealthy and have food for all.

Volume five discusses commercial taxation and economic policies from a national viewpoint. In the first part of volume six the French Revolution is discussed. A plea is made to suppress the extortion and slaying of Chinese by foreigners. "Down with Imperialism!" To realize that widely heralded slogan the Chinese must be one in spirit and in body. Then and only then will liberty and equality be attained (pp. 1-7). There follows (pp. 17-23) a critical discussion on the development of western legal conceptions and practises, concluding with the assertion that the Kuomintang will really safeguard the rights of the people, though westerners in their own countries have failed to protect their countrymen.

The seventh volume discusses Government and its administration, and describes the "Five-Power Constitution" which the Kuomintang is attempting to set up. Students are taught that only through the Kuomintang will the salvation of the people and of the nation be attained. The last volume presents the history of the Kuomintang and sets forth its program. The statement is clearly made that the Kuomintang program is uniquely Chinese being different from anything in the West. The set is rather heavy reading for children under eleven years of age.

NATIONAL READERS

XXXIII. *Tsui Hsin Ch'u Têng Hsiao Hsüeh Kuo Wên Chiao K'ê Shu* ("The New National Readers for Lower Primary Schools"). 18 vols. Shanghai: Commercial Press, 1905.*

This is the first series of readers issued by the Commercial Press to meet the demands of the new educational system inaugurated in 1905. The lessons are very practical compared with the old classics and the material is graded to suit the child's age. There are anecdotes on patriotism, filial piety, and courtesy. Many of the lessons are designed to stimulate patriotism. The tenth volume deals with China's foreign relations from the T'ang dynasty to the Boxer crisis, emphasizing the territorial losses sustained by China in the nineteenth century. The plight of the Chinese who emigrate to foreign countries is also related.

Volume nine contains a history of China's commercial intercourse with the rest of the world. A summary of the treaties is presented. These readers emphasize the existence of the treaty ports and the presence of foreign missionaries throughout the interior of the nation. By 1906, 335,000 of these readers had been published together with 67,000 of the teachers' manuals to accompany them (p. 214).

XXXIV. *New National Readers.* 10 vols. Shanghai: Commercial Press, 1904.

* Darroch, John, "Chinese Textbooks," *Journal North China Branch of the Royal Asiatic Society,* XXXVII (1906), 208-214.

A set of readers for the lower primary schools, published at the very inception of the modern educational system in China. With the establishment of the Republic it had of course to be revised. In the third volume are accounts of old Chinese customs and manners illustrated with appropriate pictures. There are several lessons on national geography. Lesson 40 states, "Soldiers are the foundation of a strong country." It continues by informing the students that bows and arrows are no longer used, but rather guns and cannons. Girls may now go to school as customs have changed in that respect.

Volume four has a lesson on China in which the question is asked, "How can we not love a country that has given us all we have?" There are lessons on the great mythological emperor Yü; on Confucius and Washington; on the defense of a city, with illustrations; illustrated lessons recounting a track-meet and a tug-of-war; on birds and animals; on Reynard the Fox; on the Boy, the Wolf and the Sheep, as well as on filial piety and friends. Volume five points out that familism prevents the development of industry in China by guarding its treasures to be bequeathed to descendents rather than investing them. The sixth volume informs us that Huang-ti invented the compass and then it was passed on to Europe! The shame of the Boxer crisis is discussed, especially the demands made on China as a result of it. The nationalists' reaction to the attempts of foreigners to build railroads and operate mines in China is forcefully recounted.

XXXV. *Chinese Primary School Readers.* 8 vols. Shanghai: Chung Hwa Press, 1912.

This set was approved by the newly reorganized Ministry of Education following the establishment of the Republic. It reached its forty-second edition within a year; in other words some 200,000 sets were sold in that time. The second volume has one lesson on soldiers and one on the flag. A lesson in volume three compares ancient and modern weapons of war, admonishing the children that all Chinese should learn how to use guns in order to protect the nation. The geography lesson points out the great size and population of China together with its flourishing wealth, and concludes of course that all Chinese should love China. One lesson, in summary fashion, recounts an attack on China, whereupon a great Chinese General waves the flag, a cannon is fired (this part is illustrated) and China wins! These lessons are judiciously placed among harmless, child-like stories, and accounts of insect and animal life.

The sixth volume has a lesson in which a man's body is likened to a nation with a unified government. There are two lessons on two of China's greatest military emperors of the past, Ch'in Shih Huang and Han Kao Tsu. There are also two lessons on Chinese geography; a lesson on Lord Nelson, with an illustration; one lesson on war and troops, and one on the Republican Memorial day and its significance. The seventh volume has three lessons on wars of one kind or another. Another lesson says that foreign control of China must be abolished before the nation can develop. There is a lesson on the territory lost by the Empire, accompanied by a map.

The content of this set of readers stands in arresting contrast to that of the classics as taught in the schools before 1905.

XXXVI. CHUANG YÜ, KAO, FENG-CH'IEN AND CHANG, YÜAN-CHI, *Republican National Readers for Higher Primary Schools.* 6 vols. Shanghai : Commercial Press, 1913.

This series fitted in exactly with the qualifications set forth by the Ministry of Education for readers soon after the establishment of the Republic and consequently bears on the cover its approval. The preface states the objects as follows :

1. The spirit of Liberty and Equality is emphasized. The virtue and method of coöperation is taught in order to cultivate a perfected personality for a Republican country.

2. The peculiar characteristics of China are presented in order to ". . . develop patriotism among our countrymen."

3. It teaches the necessity of revising the nation's old in-

jurious customs in order that the knowledge and virtue of the people may increase.

4. It defines carefully the words "State" and "Government" in order to show the value of law in the maintenance of government.

5. It advocates the equality of the five races of China in order to unify the foundations of the country.

6. It emphasizes the philanthropic spirit as do the westerners in order to increase the morality of the people.

7. It promotes physical education and a knowledge of military affairs in order to develop the militaristic spirit.

8. It emphasizes the problems relating to the people's livelihood in order to develop an independent spirit and the power of self-control.

9. It stimulates an interest in geography, history and science.

10. There are essays selected from ancient and modern writers in order to nourish an appreciation for literature.

11. It selects only simple examples of *Wên Li* (the vernacular language was not yet introduced, but a need was felt for making the classical language as simple as possible) in order that students may learn to read, but it does not use decrees and petitions issued under the Imperial régime as no Republican country would do such a thing!

XXXVII. CHUANG YÜ, *Republican National Readers for Lower Primary Schools.* 8 vols. Shanghai: Commercial Press, 1912.

A series similar in scope and viewpoint to No. XXXVI, except that it is in simpler language as it is for the lower primary pupils. The last two volumes are a good illustration of what nationalists can do even to readers. Every subject touched upon is written from the nationalistic viewpoint. Nothing is seen objectively. The whole history of China's relations with the West in the past century is reviewed with the purpose of arousing pupils to a patriotic and martial spirit.

XXXVIII. *Chinese National Language Readers.* 4 vols. Shanghai: Chung Hwa Press, 1923.

This is the teacher's handbook for the national language readers which are to be used in higher primary schools. It is written in the vernacular language. Lesson two of the first volume is on the flag. The teacher is to explain that the period of the Great Similarity, or the World Community (*Ta T'ung*), has not yet arrived, but that nationalism is the dominating force of the day and all Chinese should support their flag and their country. This viewpoint dominates fairly consistently throughout the work.

XXXIX. *New Method Series Chinese National Language Readers.* 4 vols. Shanghai: Commercial Press, 1922-23.

Volume one has five lessons relating to nationalism and international relations treating of wars, politics, and militarism. Volume two mentions the world war, Woodrow Wilson and martial bravery. The last volume has four or five lessons on national geography; the peculiar characteristics of the Chinese people; on soldiers and the duty of all Chinese to protect their country. However, all these readers, reviewed above, are but mildly nationalistic in comparison with the ones to follow which appeared as a result of the emergence of the Nationalist party into political power.

XL. Hu Chên-hui, *Hsin Shih Tai Kuo Yü Chiao K'ê Shu,* ("New Age National Readers"), 8 vols. Shanghai: Commercial Press, 1927.

This set of readers for lower primary schools was written under the supervision of Ts'ai Yüan-p'ei, sometime Chairman of the University Council, and Wong Yun-wu, Editor-in-chief of the Commercial Press. It had a large sale. Within two years the first volume reached its 290th edition; Vol. II, 240th edition; Vol. III, 180th edition; Vol. IV, 245th edition; Vol. V, 210th edition; Vol. VI, 150th edition, Vol. VII, 125th edition, Vol. VIII, 115th edition.

The contents and purposes of the set are set forth in the preface as follows:

1. The series aims to present the Kuomintang party principles and platform (T'ang I) in suitable terms to school children of the lower primary school age.

2. It forcibly presents revolutionary and progressive thought, as well as the practicality of science and of physical education for the purpose of perfecting democracy.

3. In its selection of material it aims to emphasize China's national characteristics, the spirit of independence and the individual traits of firmness, manliness and bravery.

4, 5, 6. These aims are of interest only from a pedagogical viewpoint.

Volume I

Page 10: There is a picture of the Kuomintang flag.

Volume II

Page 2: Picture of teacher and boys around Kuomintang flag, which the party aims to make the national flag of China. The teacher says the children should respect it.

Page 3: In a rhyming song on Patriotism China is likened to a precious jewel whom all with united heart should love and protect.

Volume III

Page 4: The lesson is a conversation between the teacher and the students as to what a "lost country" is. The teacher informs the students that they can lose their country if they do not love it.

Page 5: The teacher praises the student who says he will fight for his country if anyone comes to molest it.

Page 20: The lesson is on the significance of October tenth, the anniversary of the establishment of the Republic.

Page 21: The children are told how they should celebrate Republican independence day in the home. They should draw a picture of Sun Yat-sen, make a flag and hang them together on the wall.

Page 22: This lesson recounts Sun's life.

Page 23: Another lesson on Sun, the "Father of his Country."

Page 45: The difference between foreign and Chinese goods is pointed out with the obvious moral, that if you love your country you will buy Chinese goods.

Volume IV

Page 6: A lesson on George Washington and the American Revolution.

Page 11: This lesson says that students should sacrifice themselves to preserve equality of social relationships.

Page 23: This lesson says that Washington didn't tell a lie, though Ssu-ma Kwang, one of China's great scholars did! It is better to be like George Washington.

Volume V

Page 11: Here is a revolutionary song extolling the Republic and condemning the unequal treaties and foreign economic aggression.

Pages 14-15: "The Nation's Shame" arises out of the Opium War, the taking of Hongkong and the opening of the Yangtze river to foreign shipping.

Pages 16-18: Continuation of the above lesson. The nation's shame is also due to the seizure of Annam by France, of Burma by England and of Korea and Taiwan by Japan; also because of the entrance of the Allied troops into Peking in 1900, of the occupation of the treaty ports, the May 30th Incident and the Twenty-one Demands.

Page 19: A song titled "Remove the Nation's Shame." It teaches the children that by making their bodies strong, working hard, having a brave and resolute spirit they can, if they are willing to sacrifice their bodies and their minds, do not fear death, and are willing to fight, remove the nation's shame.

Page 21: This lesson says that opium smoking came from the West.

Page 50: Sun Yat-sen's will is presented.

Volume VI

Pages 3-5: Lessons on Revolutionary heroes are presented.

Page 11: The life of Chiang Chieh-shih, the Generalissimo of Nationalist China is recounted.

Page 12: A brief account of Sun's childhood is presented.

Pages 17-18: Some pictures revealing the nature of the nation's shame followed by discussions.

Pages 31-32: A little poem is presented urging the children to use only "Patriotic Cloth" and not any of foreign make.

Pages 38-40: A favorable account of the T'ai-p'ing Rebellion is here presented. The nationalists have decided to use this historic episode of the nineteenth century as a forerunner of their own revolution. For that reason no mention is made of the influence of Christianity on the movement. Earlier accounts in textbooks and elsewhere tended to discredit the movement and therefore lay the blame for its origin at the door of the Christian missionary. This present account commends the T'ai-p'ings on their recognition of the equality of women.

Pages 47-48: A little song is here given setting forth the Three Principles of the People (San Min Chu I).

Pages 50-52: This lesson discusses the evils of opium smoking which Great Britain forced on China.

Pages 55-56: This lesson is a plea for the militarization of China in order to abolish the unequal treaties.

Volume VII

Pages 4-5: Sun Yat-sen is called the successor of Hung Hsiuch'üan, the leader of the T'ai-p'ing Movement.

Many pages in this volume are devoted to lessons on old Chinese generals and war heroes. The purpose no doubt is to realize one of the major purposes set forth in the preface—to call forth the qualities of bravery and manliness. Military heroes presumably best exemplify these cherished virtues.

Volume VIII

Pages 4-5: The death of Sun Yat-sen is recounted and his public and private wills presented.

Pages 6-8: The Three Principles of the People are explained.

Page 27: The story of the 300 Spartan braves is recounted.

Pages 31-33: This lesson very adroitly makes patriotic sentiment out of the defeat sustained by China at Shimonoseki where the peace treaty of 1895 was signed.

Pages 40-42: The history of the patriotic "Five-four Movement" (May 4, 1919) is told, and reference is made to Woodrow Wilson's principle of self-determination.

Pages 52-54: The nature of political and economic imperialism, as it operates in China, is revealed.

Pages 54-57: A résumé of the French Revolution and its spread under Napoleon. It is pointed out that the French Republic was not established until eighty to ninety years after the Revolution and the Chinese should take heart in that fact.

Pages 58-60: Here we find discussed the origin of the "Marseillaise." A partial translation is given and the relation of the song to the French Revolution is traced.

In all some sixty, out of 430, pages of material are devoted to subjects the immediate aim of which is to stimulate the spirit of nationalism. The amount of space devoted to this type of propaganda tends to increase from volume to volume until it fills one-third of the space in the last one. Furthermore, many more pages recount the history of military heroes of China's past in order to arouse a martial spirit among the youth. We find little that relates the child to his family and community life or presents the problems that arise therefrom. Moreover, there is nothing to arouse in him a sense of his duties and responsibilities to the World Community and to mankind. A distorted view of the problems of life, such as this, is one of the most striking weaknesses of Nationalism, and therein lies its greatest harm. The emphasis placed on the French Revolution may be directly attributed to Ts'ai Yüan-p'ei's influence. He was educated in part in France and in educational matters ever leans in that direction.

XLI. Hu, Chên-hui, *Hsin Shih Tai Kuo Yü Chiao K'ê Shu,* ("New Age National Readers for Higher Primary Schools") 4 vols. Shanghai: Commercial Press, 1927; 70th ed., 1928.

Over three hundred thousand sets of these readers were sold in one year to 600,000 students in higher primary schools. This set aims to do for these more advanced students what the set number XL, reviewed above, does for the lower primary school students.

Volume I

Page 1: There is a song on the national flag right at the outset.

Pages 16-18: Here a Korean nationalist voices in poetic form his aspiration for the attainment of Korean independence.

Pages 46-51: The whole subject of the Boxer crisis and the indignities suffered by the Chinese at the hands of the foreigners is here set forth.

Volume II

Pages 14-16: Here we find the Whampoa Military Academy, China's West Point, described.

Pages 17-19: Gandhi's non-coöperative movement is sympathetically narrated.

Pages 20-22: Yüeh Fei, China's great general and irredentist, is here presented as a hero worthy of worship by twentieth-century Chinese children.

Pages 36-38: Sun Yat-sen's virtues are extolled in these pages.

Pages 38-40: Various aspects of the history of the Kuomintang are here narrated.

Volume IV

Pages 1-2: The ill-treatment which the Chinese emigrants in the Nanyang areas (Philippines, British Malaya, Annam and

Dutch East Indies) receive at the hands of the white man is here graphically recounted and the fact that the Chinese government is unable to protect them is lamented.

Pages 2-11: The same subject is continued, going more into detail as to the extent of the white man's control of the area and concluding with an account of the policy of the Japanese government in driving out the Chinese traders in that area.

Pages 14-18: The third of the Three Principles of the People, the question of the People's Livelihood, is here discussed.

Pages 48-50: Here again the problem of the Chinese emigrants is presented. It was drawn from one of Liang Ch'i-ch'ao's essays on the subject.

GEOGRAPHY TEXTS

XLII. ZAI, HONG LAI, *Complete Geography with Coloured Maps.* Shanghai : Commercial Press, 1903.

This geography, which was designed for advanced classes in schools and for the general reader, was compiled by a member of the Anglo-Chinese College in Shanghai. It had the approval of the Imperial official who was in general charge of school affairs at that time. In his introduction the author informs us that he has selected his material from a number of books on Chinese geography published both in China and in the West. He aims to stress the importance of racial conflict and competition in order to arouse the spirit of his Chinese readers. He commences with a general discussion of the world from a physical viewpoint, then of the peoples on it and their various languages and concludes with an outline of the various stages in the development of civilizations which are moving toward the ultimate goal of the world community *(Ta T'ung Chih Shih).*

The nation is defined as being a stage on the way to the world community. It is composed of a group of people inhabiting a fixed area in whom is invested the sovereign right to promulgate laws with which to defend itself.

XLIII. Tu Chi, *Chung Kuo Ti Li Chung Hsüeh Chiao K'ê Shu* ("A Geographical Study of the Chinese Empire"). Shanghai: Commercial Press, 1906.

This text, for use in middle schools, was prepared by a professor of geography and history in the Imperial University of Peking. He says in his preface that there is need of a good geography for Chinese students, as those prepared by the foreigners—for the most part missionaries—are not suitable for the education of the nation's students. He wants, therefore, to write a real national geography. He says, "In order to have a nation it is necessary to have a group of people inhabiting a fixed area and having definitely defined rights." This definition comes from one of Liang Ch'i-ch'iao's essays. He feels that it is the province of geography to show to the people its relations to their characteristics and to their rights. However ardent his intentions were he did not succeed in writing as forcible and clearcut a nationalistic treatise as did his successors.

XLIV. Chuang Yü, *Kung Ho Kuo Chiao K'ê Shu-Hsin Ti Li* ("Chinese Geography"). 6 vols. Shanghai: Commercial Press, 1913.

This series for use in higher primary schools had the approval of the Ministry of Education. In connection with a description of Macao and Hongkong the author says, "What a pity it is that these places, as important to the nation as the windpipe is to man should be in the control of other men!" (p. 4.) While recounting the geography of Yunnan he carefully points out how difficult it is to defend it now that England has seized Burma and France, Annam. He says that these countries have even built railroads to consolidate their hold. China must be on its guard. A whole chapter is devoted to the leased areas. Mention is made of Chinese emigrants in the Nanyang area.

The last two volumes deal with the world in general. Mankind is divided into the antiquated and meaningless five categories based on color. "In the world of today," writes the author, "the yellow race is very important. The white race is very strong and few are they who do not fall under its control" (pp. 16, 17).

XLV. *Chinese Geography for Middle Schools.* 4 vols. Shanghai, Chung Hwa Press, 1915.

This set had the approval of the Ministry of Education. In its preface the author states that this book advocates militarism as the nation is not yet strongly founded. In the introduction of political propaganda these geographies become a means of creating the nationalistic type of citizen.

XLVI. TING CH'A, *Hsin Chung Hsüeh Chiao K'ê Shu-Ch'u Chi Pên Kuo Ti Li* ("Chinese Geography"). 2 vols. Shang-hai: Chung Hwa Press, 1923.

This geography for use in junior middle schools had the ap-proval of the Ministry of Education. Twenty-three editions were published in five years. It is highly nationalistic, taking every opportunity to put before the students China's contemporary and very temporary political situations. A whole section which is devoted to foreign relations, closes with an eloquent passage depicting the glory of one of the world's richest and largest nations being utterly desecrated by the "barbarians" (II, 194). The character for barbarian "I" was only finally driven out of diplomatic documents as a result of two wars, but now it has crept back into this little textbook on geography under the in-fluence of nationalism. So much space is devoted in the text to describing political situations that the student is deprived of much real knowledge concerning the actual nature of his own country from a geographical viewpoint.

XLVII. CHU, WÊN-SHU AND CHÊNG CH'ANG, *Hsin Hsüeh Chih Ti Li K'ê Pên* ("New Educational System Geography Read-ers"). 4 vols. Shanghai, Chung Hwa Press, 1923.

This set for use in higher primary schools reached a sale of 90,000 copies in four years. In the first volume, after reviewing the effects of western imperialism on China, the author says this must be stopped and China's rights restored (p. 2). The geo-graphical description of Manchuria concerns itself primarily with the position of the Japanese in that area. In the second volume, in connection with the loss of Formosa to Japan, is quoted the old proverb, "When the lips are lost the teeth become cold" (p. 25). China's ten million emigrants are too precious to be under the control of other men (p. 27). After making a broad survey of the relation to each other of the powers in the Pacific ocean the author concludes by asserting that China, with its great size and wealth, will some day become master of the Pacific and only then will the Pacific become in reality what it is now only in name (pp. 28-29).

The third and fourth volumes are only cursive, journalistic treatments of all the other countries, touching only on the super-ficialities and concluding by comparing one country with an-other, finally deploring China's present status. It is political geography pure and simple. The child will gain the impression that changes in national boundaries are the chief concern and end of man and that these changes come about only through war. A more inadequate geography text from every point of view it would be impossible to conceive.

XLVIII. Wang, Chung-ch'i, *Hsien Tai Ch'u Chung Hsüeh Chiao K'ê Shu-Pên Kuo Ti Li.* ("The Geography of China"). 2 vols. Shanghai: Commercial Press, 1923.

This text is for use in junior middle schools. The first volume is devoted to a general objective treatment of man's relation to nature and the second volume to a detailed description of Chinese geography. Though much better than the text reviewed just above, it is a general *mèlange* of historical and political facts discussing, for example, the wars with England, France and Japan. Several pages are devoted to the army and navy.

As a general rule in the geography texts it is only when dealing with China that political material such as this is introduced.

APPENDIX II

A list of the Chinese characters used in this work.

Chang Chih-tung	張 之 洞
Chang Chiu-ju	張 九 如
Chang Pai-hsi	張 百 熙
Chang Yüan-chi	張 元 濟
Chao Êrh-hsün	趙 爾 巽
Ch'ên Ch'i-t'ien	陳 啟 天
Ch'ên Pao-ch'üan	陳 寶 泉
Ch'ên Tu-hsiu	陳 獨 秀
Chêng Ch'ang	鄭 昶
Chêng Wu Ch'u	政 務 處
Chi Fên Shêng Shê	積 分 卅 舍
Chi Ho Yüan Pên	幾 何 原 本
Chi Szŭ	禊 祀
Chiang Chieh-shih (Kai-shek)	蔣 介 石

Chiang Monlin
(Mêng-lin) 蔣夢麟

Chiao Yü Kung Pao 教育公報

Chiao Yü Pu Ling
Hui Pien 教育部令彙編

Chiao Yü Pu Pien
Tsuan Ku Yüeh K'an 教育部編纂股月刊

Chiao Yü Pu Wên Tu
Hui Pien 教育部文牘彙編

Chiao Yü Shang Ti
Kuo Chia Chu I Yü
Ch'i T'a San Chung
Chu I Chih Pi Chiao 教育上的國家主義與其他三種主義之比較

Chiao Yü Shih Chieh 教育世界

Chiao Yü Tsa Chih 教育雜誌

Chiao Yü Ts'ung Shu
Ch'u Chi 教育叢書初集

Ch'ien Lung 乾隆

Ch'ien Tzǔ K'ê Hsiu
Shên Yung Pên 千字課修身用本

Chih 志

Chihli-Chou 直隸州

Chin Ch'êng Jih Pên
  Ming Chih Pien
  Chêng K'ao Hsü 進呈日本明治變政考序

Chin Pu Tang 進步黨

Ch'iu Shih Huang Ti 秦始皇帝

Chin Tai Chung Kuo
  Chiao Yü Shih Liao 近代中國教育史料

Ch'in Ting Ch'u Têng
  Hsiao Hsüeh T'ang
  Chang Chêng 欽定初等小學堂章程

Ch'in Ting Chung Hsüeh
  T'ang Chang Chêng 欽定中學堂章程

Ch'in Ting Szŭ K'u
  Ch'üan Shu Tsung Mu 欽定四庫全書總目

Ching Chi Chih 經籍志

Ching Pao 京報

Ching Pu I 經部一

Ch'ing Shih Kao 清史稿

Ch'ing Shih Kuan Shu
  Chü Yin 清史館書局印

Chiu Chang 九章

Chou 周

Chou Chih-kan 周之淦

Chou Fa 周法

Chou Fu 周馥

Chou Kuan 周官

Chou Tso-jên 周作人

Chu Ching-nêng (nung) 朱經農

Chu Hsi 朱熹

Chü-jên 舉人

Chu Tzǔ-ch'ên 朱子辰

Chu Wên-shu 朱文叔

Chüan 卷

Ch'üan Kuo Chiao Yü Hui I Pao Kao 全國教育會議報告

Chuang Yü 莊俞

Chün 軍

Ch'ün Chi Ch'üan Chieh Lun 羣己權界論

Ch'un Ch'iu 春秋

Ch'ün Hsüeh I Yen　群學肄言

Chung Hsi Hsüeh T'ang　中西學堂

Chung hsüeh wei chu;
　hsi hsüeh wei yung　中學為主
　　　　　　　　　　西學為用

Chung Hua (Hwa) Chiao
　Yü Chieh　中華教育界

Chung Kuo Chiao Yü Chêng
　Ts'ê　中國教育政策

Chung Kuo Hsin Chiao Yü
　Szŭ Ch'ao Hsiao Shih　中國新教育思潮小史

Chung Kuo Pao Hsüeh Shih　中國報學史

Chung Kuo Ti Li Chung
　Hsüeh Chiao K'ê Shu　中國地理中學教科書

Chung Yung　中庸

Fa　法

Fa Chia　法家

Fa I　法意

Fan Ping-ch'ing　樊炳清

Fan Yüan-lien　范源廉

Fu　府

Hai Kuo T'u Chih　海國圖志

Hanlin 翰林

Han Wên Shu Kuan 漢文書館

Hsi Yü T'ung Wên Chih 西域同文志

Hsi Hsüeh K'ao Lüeh 西學考畧

Hsiang Hsüeh Hsin Pao 湘學新報

Hsiao Hsüeh 小學

Hsiao Hsüeh Lei 小學類

Hsien 縣

Hsien Fêng 咸豐

Hsien Tai Ch'u Chung
Chiao K'ê Shu Pên
Kuo Shih
現代初中教科書本國史

Hsin Chiao Yü 新教育

Hsin Chih Hsiu Shên
Chiao Pên
新制修身教本

Hsin Chuan Ch'u Chi
Chung Hsüeh Chiao K'ê
Shu Kung Min
新撰初級中學教科書公民

Hsin Chuan Ch'u Chi
Chung Hsüeh Chiao K'ê
Shu Shih Chieh Shih
新撰初級中學教科書世界史

Hsin Chung Hsüeh Chiao
K'ê Shu Ch'u Chi-Kung
Min K'ê Pên
新中學教科書初級公民課本

Hsin Chung Hsüeh Chiao 新中學教科書
    K'ê Shu Ch'u Chi-Pên 初級本國地理
    Kuo Ti Li

Hsin Chung Hsüeh Chih 新中學制
    Ti Li K'ê Pên 地理課本

Hsin Kuo Chia Chu I Yü 新國家主義與
    Kuo Min Chiao Yü Ti 國民教育的改
    Kai Tsao 造

Hsin Min Pao 新民報

Hsin Min Ts'ung Pao 新民叢報會
    Hui

Hsin Shih Tai Hsiu Shên 新時代修
    Chiao K'ê Shu 身教科書

Hsin Shih Tai Kuo Yü 新時代國
    Chiao K'ê Shu 語教科書

Hsin Shih Tai Li Shih 新時代歷
    Chiao K'ê Shu 史教科書

Hsin Shih Tai Pên Kuo 新時代本國
    Shih Chiao K'ê Shu 史教科書

Hsin Shih Tai San Min 新時代三民
    Chu I Chiao K'ê Shu 主義教科書

Hsin Shih Tai San Min 新時代三民
    Chu I Chiao Pên 主義教本

Hsiu Shên 修身

Hsü Kuang-ch'i 徐光啟

Hsüan Chü 選舉

Hsüan Chü Chih 選舉誌

Hsüeh Pu 學部

Hsüeh T'ang 學堂

Hsüeh Wu Ch'u 學務處

Hu An Yü Chiao Yü 滬案與教育

Hu Chên-hui 胡貞惠

Hu Pao 滬報

Hu Shih 胡適

Hu Yu-chih 胡愈之

Hua Chih An 花之安

Huang Ti 黃帝

Hung Hsiu-ch'üan 洪秀全

I 夷

I Ching 易經

Jên Ts'ai 人才

Kai Chêng Nêng Min Ch'ien Tzŭ K'ê 改正農民千字課

Kana; Hirakana; Katakana 假名, 平假名 片假名

Kao, Fêng-ch'ien 高鳳謙

K'ang Hsi 康熙

K'ang Nan Hai Wên Chi 康南海文集

K'ang Yu-wei 康有為

K'ao Shih 考試

Kiangnan Chih Tsao Chü Chi 江南製造局記

K'iuen Hio P'ien 勸學篇

K'o Chü 科舉

Ko Kung-chên 戈公振

Kuan Hua 官話

Kuan Yü 關羽

Kuang Fang Yen Kuan 廣方言館

Ku Chieh-kang 顧頡剛

Kung (Prince) 恭王

Kung Ho Kuo Chiao K'ê
Shu Hsiu Shên Yao I 共和國教科書修身要義

Kung Min 公民

Kung Min Hsü Chih 公民須知

Kung Min Hsüeh K'ê
Ch'êng Ta Kang 公民學課程大綱

Kung Min Mo Fan 公民模範

Kuo Chia Chu I Yü
Chiao Yü 國家主義與教育

Kuo Min 國民

Kuo Min Pi Tu 國民必讀

Kuomintang 國民黨

Kuo Ping-wên 郭秉文

Kuo-yü 國語

Kuang Hsü (Kwang) 光緒

Kuang Hsü Chêng Yao (Kwang) 光緒政要

Kuang Hsü Tung Hua Hsü
Lu (Kwang) 光緒東華續錄

Li　禮

Li Chi　禮記

Li Hung-chang　李鴻章

Li Pu　禮部

Li Pu-ch'ing　李步青

Li Shan-lan　李善蘭

Li Tuan-fen　李端芬

Li Yang　李楊

Liang Ch'i-ch'ao　梁啓超

Liu Fu　劉復

Liu K'un-i　劉坤一

Liu Kang-hou　劉康侯

Lo Chên-yü　羅振玉

Lun Yü　論語

Ma Chien-chung　馬建忠

Ma Chih Wên T'ung　馬氏文通

Mêng-tzŭ　孟子

Min-ch'üan　民權

Min-shêng　民生

Min-tsu 民族

Ming 明

Ming Hsüeh Ch'ien Shuo 名學淺說

Mu Lê Ming Hsüeh 穆勒名學

Nan Hsüeh Hui 南學會

Nan Yang Kung Hsüeh 南洋公學

Pa Ku 八股

Pa Ku Wên Chang 八股文章

Pai Hua 白話

P'an Wên-an 潘文安

Pei Yang Hsi Hsüeh 北洋西學

Pei Yang Ta Ch'ên 北洋大臣

Pien Pao-ch'üan 邊寶泉

P'in-hsing 品行

P'ing Min Ch'ien Tzŭ K'e 平民千字課

San Min Chu I 三民主義

San Min Chu I Chiao Yü Hsüeh 三民主義與教育學

Shang Wu 尚武

Shang Yeh Tao Tê 商業道德

Shê Hui Tung Ch'üan 社會通詮

Shên Pao 申報

Shên Pao-chên 沈葆楨

Shêng Hsüan-huai 盛宣懷

Shêng Tsai-hsiang 盛在珦

Shih 史

Shih Chieh Ta T'ung 世界大同

Shih Ching 詩經

Shih Min Ch'ien Tzŭ K'e 市民千字課

Shih Ping Ch'ien Tzŭ K'e 士兵千字課

Shou Hui Chiao Yü Ch'üan Yün Tung 收回教育權運動

Shu Ching 書經

Shu Hsin-ch'êng 舒新城

Shu Li Ching Yün 數理精蘊

Shu Yüan 書院

Ssu-ma Kuang 司馬光

Sui Shih 隋史

Sun Chia-nai 孫家鼐

Sun Yat-sen 孫逸仙

Sung Shih 宋史

Szŭ Shu 四書

Szŭ T'u 司徒

Ta 大

Ta Ch'êng Kuan 大成館

Ta Ch'ing Lü Li 大清律例

Ta Ching Lü Li Hui Chi Pien Lan 大清律例彙輯便覽

Ta Fu 大夫

Ta Hsüeh 大學

Ta Hsüeh Yüan 大學院

Ta T'ung 大同

Ta T'ung Chih Shih 大同之世

T'ai Hsi Hsüeh Hsaio Lun Lüeh 泰西學校論署

T'ai-p'ing 太平

T'ai Hsü 太虛

Tang Hua 黨化

T'ang Hua-lung 湯化龍

T'ao Chih-hsing 陶知行

T'ao Hui-tsêng 陶彙曾

Tao-t'ai 道臺

Tao-tê 道德

Tê Kuo Hsüeh Hsiao Lun Lüeh 德國學校論署

T'ien Yen Lun 天演論

T'ing 廳

Ting Ch'a 丁詧

Ting Hsien 定縣

Ts'ai Yüan-pei 蔡元培

Tsên Ch'un-hsüan 岑春瑄

Tsêng Kuo-fan 曾國藩

Tso Tsung-t'ang 左宗棠

Tsui Hsin Ch'u Têng Hsiao Hsüeh Hsiu Shên Chiao K'ê Shu 最新初等小學修身教科書

Tsui Hsin Ch'u Têng Hsiao Hsüeh Kuo Wên Chiao K'ê Shu 最新初等小學國文教科書

Tsungli Yamen 總理衙門

Tuan Fang 端方

Tu-chün 督軍

T'ung Chien Kang Mu 通鑑鋼目

T'ung Hua 同化

Tung Hua Hsü Lu 東華續錄

Tung Hua Lu 東華錄

T'ung Mêng Hui 同盟會

T'ung Wên Kuan 同文館

Tzŭ Ch'iang 自強

Tz'ŭ Yüan 辭源

Wan Kwoh (Kuo) Kung Pao 萬國公報

Wang Kuo-wei	王國維
Wang Wên-shao·	王文韶
Wei Yüan	魏源
Wên Chang	文章
Wêng Chang-chung	翁長鐘
Wong Yün-wu	王雲五
Wu Ching	五經
Wu Pei Hsüeh T'ang	武備學堂
Yamen	衙門
Yen Fu	嚴復
Yen Hsi-shan	閻錫山
Yen I Ming Chu Ts'ung K'an	嚴譯名著叢刊
Yin Ping Shih Wên Chi Ch'üan Pien	飲冰室文集全編
Yin Yang Wên	陰陽文
Yü Chia-chü	余家菊
Yüan Fu	原富
Yüan Shih-k'ai	袁世凱
Yüeh (Yo)-fei	岳飛
Yung Chêng	雍正
Yung Wing	容閎

BIBLIOGRAPHY

A Select

List of the Works Found Most Useful

in the

Preparation of This Book

Books, Pamphlets and Official Collections

Brunnert, N. S. and Hagelstrom, V. V. (Trans. from the Russian by Beltchenko, A., and Moran, E. E.), Present Day Political Organization of China, Shanghai, 1912.

Chao, Êr-hsüan *et al.*, Ch'ing Shih Kao ("Draft History of the Ch'ing Dynasty"). 131 vols. Peking, 1928.

Chiang, Monlin, A Study in the Chinese Principles of Education. Shanghai, 1924.

Chiao Yü Pu Wên Tu Hui Pien (Collected Documents published from time to time by the Ministry of Education after 1912).

Chiao Yü Ta Tzŭ Shu ("The Chinese Cyclopedia of Education"). 2 vols., Shanghai, 1928-1930.

Chinese National Association for the Advancement of Education, Bulletins. Vol. II, Peking, 1923.

Chu, Ch'ou-p'êng (Ed.), Kwang Hsü Tung Hua Hsü Lu (Collection of official documents, 1874-1908). 64 vols., Shanghai, 1909.

Chung Shan Ts'ung Shu (Collected works of Sun Yat-sen). 4 vols., Shanghai, 1928.

Cordier, Henri, Bibliotheca Sinica. Dictionnaire bibliographique des ouvrages relatifs à l'empire Chinois. 2nd Ed., 4 vols. and a sup., Paris, 1923.

Duyvendak, J. J. L., *Over Chineesche Oorlogsgoden*, Leyden, 1919.

Franke, O., Ostasiatische Neubildungen. Beiträge zum Verstandnis der politischen und kulturellen Entwicklungs-Vorgänge im Fernen Osten, Hamburg, 1911.

GRAYBILL, HENRY B., The Educational Reform in China. Hongkong, 1911.

HAIL, WILLIAM JAMES, Tsêng Kuo-fan and the T'aip'ing Rebellion. New Haven, 1927.

HAYES, CARLTON J. H., Essays on Nationalism. New York, 1926.

———, The Historical Evolution of Modern Nationalism. New York, 1931.

KING, H. E., The Educational System of China as Recently Reconstructed. United States Bureau of Education, Bulletin 15, Whole Number 469. Washington, 1911.

KO, KUNG-CHÊN, Chung Kuo Pao Hsüeh Shih ("History of Chinese Journalism"). 2nd Ed., Shanghai, 1928.

KUO, PING-WÊN, The Chinese System of Public Education. New York, 1914.

LEW, T. T., et al., China Today through Chinese Eyes. London, 1st ser., 1922; 2d ser., 1926.

LIU, FU, Les Mouvements de la Langue Nationale en Chine. Paris, 1925.

LO, R. Y., China's Revolution from the Inside. New York, 1930.

MARTIN, W. A. P., A Cycle of Cathay. New York, 1896.

MAYBON, ALBERT, La Politique Chinoise. Paris, 1908.

MAYERS, W. F., The Chinese Government. Shanghai, 1886.

MONROE, PAUL, Report on Education in China. Bulletin of the Institute of International Education. New York, 1922.

MORSE, H. B., The International Relations of the Chinese Empire. 3 vols., London, 1910-18.

SHÊN, T'UNG-SHÊNG, TUNG YÜAN AND TUNG JUN (Ed.), Kwang Hsü Chêng Yao. (A select collection of official documents, 1874-1908.) 30 vols., Nan Yang Kuan Shu Chü, Shanghai, 1909.

SHU, HSIN-CH'ÊNG, Shou Hui Chiao Yü Ch'üan Yün Tung ("Restore-the-Educational-Prerogatives Movement"). Shanghai, 1927.

SHU, HSIN-CH'ÊNG (Ed.) Chin Tai Chung Kuo Chiao Yü Shih Liao (A collection of documents on the history of education in China in modern times). 4 vols., Shanghai, 1928.

STAUFFER, M. T. (Ed.), The Christian Occupation of China. Shanghai, 1922.

STEIGER, G. N., China and the Occident: The Origin and Development of the Boxer Movement. New Haven, 1927.

SUN YAT-SEN, San Min Chu I ("Three Principles of the People"). Trans. by Frank W. Price, ed. by L. T. Chen, Shanghai, 1927.

T'ANG, LEANG-LI, China in Revolt. How a Civilization Became a Nation. London, 1927.

THE UNIVERSITY COUNCIL (Comp.), Ch'üan Kuo Chiao Yü Hui I Pao Kao, ("National Educational Conference Report"). Shanghai, 1928.

TOBAR, PÈRE JÉROME (Trans.), K'iuen-Hio P'ien (Exhortations à l'étude par S. Exc. Tchang Tche-tong). Shanghai, 1909.

T'ZŬ YÜAN ("Encyclopedia"). Shanghai. Numerous editions.

WANG, TSI, C., The Youth Movement in China. New York, 1927.

WOODBRIDGE, SAMUEL I., China's Only Hope. New York, 1900.

YIN, CHILING, Reconstruction of Modern Educational Organizations in China. Shanghai, 1924.

YUNG, WING, My Life in China and America. New York, 1909.

ZI, PÈRE ETIENNE, Pratique des Examens Littéraires en Chine. Shanghai, 1894.

PERIODICALS

CHIAO YÜ KUNG PAO (Monthly publication of the Ministry of Education). Peking and Nanking, 1912 et seq.

CHIAO YÜ SHIH CHIEH ("The Educational World"), about April, 1901 to 1909.

CHIAO YÜ TSA CHIH ("Chinese Educational Review"). Shanghai, 1909 et seq.

CHUNG HUA CHIAO YÜ CHIEH ("Chung Hua Educational Review"). Shanghai, 1913 et seq.

EAST OF ASIA. Shanghai, 1902-1906.

HSIN CHIAO YÜ ("The New Education"). Shanghai, 1919 et seq.

JOURNAL OF THE NORTH CHINA BRANCH OF THE ROYAL ASIATIC SOCIETY. Shanghai, 1858 et seq.

NEW CHINA REVIEW. Shanghai, 1919 1922.

THE CHINESE RECORDER, Published at Foochow in 1867 as The Missionary Recorder, at Foochow in 1868-1872 as The Chinese Recorder and Missionary Journal, and at Shanghai 1874 et seq. About 1911 name was shortened to The Chinese Recorder.

THE CHINA REVIEW, OR NOTES AND QUERIES ON THE FAR EAST. Hongkong, 1872-1901.

T'OUNG PAO: Archives pour servir a l'étude de l'histoire, des langues, de la géographie et de l'ethnographie de l'Asie Orientale, Leiden, 1890 et seq.

NOTES AND REFERENCES

CHAPTER I

1. The characters for Chinese names, titles of books, references, etc. will be found in App. II.
2. Ly-Chao-Pee, "Le Progrès en Chine," *Journal des Economistes,* Nov., 1881, p. 7; *Ch'ing Shih Kao,* ("Draft History of the Ch'ing Dynasty") Hsüan Chü, Chih 2, pp. 1, 2.
3. Martin, W. A. P., *A Cycle of Cathay,* p. 301; *Ch'ing Shih Kao,* Hsüan Chü, Chih 2, pp. 1, 2.
4. Shu, Hsin-ch'êng, *Chin Tai Chung Kuo Chiao Yü Shih Liao* ("A Collection of Documents on the History of Education in China in Modern Times"), Vol. I, sec. 2, pp. 7-9; *Draft History of the Ch'ing Dynasty,* Hsüan Chü, Chih 2, pp. 1, 2; Martin, *op. cit.,* pp. 302-3.
5. Hail, W. J., *Tsêng Kuo-fan and the T'aip'ing Rebellion,* p. 370.
6. *Chi Ho Yüan Pên,* the complete text of Euclid in Chinese; the first six chapters being a reprint of Matteo Ricci's work (edition 1611) and the nine remaining chapters being a translation by Alexander Wylie and Li Shan-lan. Printed in 1865 with a preface by Tsêng Kuo-fan. There is in the David Eugene Smith collection on Mathematics at Columbia University a manuscript also called *Chi Ho Yüan Pên.* As the prefaces explain, it is a translation of the first six chapters of Euclid, orally explained by Matteo Ricci and put in writing by Hsü Kuang-ch'i. The work was printed in 1607. A postface written by Hsü relates that after Ricci's death a printed copy with corrections in his own handwriting was found. Assisted by two friends Hsü prepared a revised edition in 1611 of which this is a copy. (Cp. Moule, G. E., "The Obligations of China to Europe in the Matter of Physical Sciences acknowledged by Eminent Chinese," *Journal of the North China Branch of the Royal Asiatic Society,* New Ser. no. VII (1873), 147-64.) In this connection also see

the *Shu Li Ching Yün* which was published by Imperial order in 1723, giving a comprehensive summary of the science of mathematics incorporating all the recent Western developments. It contains the earliest description of European algebra and the earliest complete treatise on logarithms in Chinese. The table of logarithms appears to be a transcript of Vlacq's tables, published in Holland in 1628. For further evidence of the influence of European science and thought on the Chinese in this early period see Wei Yuan's, *Hai Kuo T'u Chih* ("Descriptive and Historical Geography of Foreign Countries"), 100 chüan in 24 volumes. In his preface the author acknowledges the sources from which he drew his information including the works of the missionaries Matteo Ricci, J. Aléni, F. Verbiest, and others. The third and fourth volumes contain more than seventy-five maps. The last chapter discusses the construction of ships of war, of steam vessels, firearms, astronomy, etc.

7. The preface was actually composed by his son, Tsêng Hui-min as appears from a collection of the latter's works where the preface is reprinted with the note: "written for my father."

8. Moule, *op. cit.,* p. 158. Also see Hail, *op. cit.,* pp. 303-4 and Yung Wing, *My Life in China and America,* pp. 138 *et seq.* especially pp. 148-53 and pp. 168-69. These passages recount Yung Wing's interviews with Tsêng Kuo-fan at Anking. As a result the Viceroy ordered Yung Wing to go to America to buy machinery. This was set up at Shanghai and formed the Kiangnan arsenal. The first steamer built in China was constructed there and launched in 1868. Viceroy Tsêng added a mechanical school to the arsenal at Yung Wing's suggestion. One of the letters asking Yung Wing to come to Anking to confer with Tsêng was from "Li Sien Lan" or Li Shan-lan (*vide supra,* Note 6), the mathematician.

9. The *Chiu Chang,* or the Nine Sections of Chinese mathematics, are as follows: 1. Plane mensuration, 2. Proportion, 3. Fellowship or the apportioning of taxes paid by the rich and the poor, 4. Evolution, 5. Solid mensuration, 6. Alligation, 7. Calculation of profit and loss, 8. Equations, 9. Trigonometry. See Alexander Wylie in the *Chinese and Japanese Repository* for May, 1864 for a lengthy article on this subject.

10. Cordier, Henri, *L'Imprimerie Sino-Européenne en Chine,* Bibli-

ographie des ouvrages publiés en Chine par les Européens au XVIIe et XVIIIe siècle, Paris, 1901. Out of several hundred extant works published by about eighty missionaries during this period, fourteen were devoted to transmitting western science and mathematics to the Chinese. They published in all some 71 works: 4 on geography, 12 on geometry, arithmetic and trigonometry; 11 on science and machinery in general, and 44 on astronomy.

11. Among the means employed by the Jesuit Fathers to ingratiate themselves at the Chinese Court was that of instruction in the art of casting cannon.

12. Zi, Etienne, Le Père, *Pratique des examens littéraires en Chine*, p. 115.

13. Martin, W. A. P., *op. cit.*, p. 318.

14. Zi, *op, cit.*, p. 115.

15. Fryer, John, "Chinese Education—Past, Present and Future," *Chinese Recorder*, XVIII (1897), 381-82.

16. *Kiangnan Chih Tsao Chü Chi*, (History of the Kiangnan Arsenal), 10 chüan, Shanghai: Fu Hai Li Wên Pao Shu Chü, Sept., 1905, chüan 2, pp. 15-23; p. 31A.

17. The Chinese Library of Columbia University has 107 of these translated works.

18. Fryer, John, *op. cit.*, p. 382.

19. *Ibid.; Draft History of the Ch'ing Dynasty*, Hsüan Chü, Chih 2, pp. 1, 2.

20. *Kuang Hsü Chêng Yao* (A select collection of important documents made from the official collection *Kuang Hsü Tung Hua Hsü Lu* covering the years 1875-1908), chüan 11, pp. 10, 11.

21. Hail, *op. cit.*, pp. 1-6.

22. Shu, Hsin-ch'êng, *op. cit.*, I, 22 *et seq.*

23. Ly-Chao-Pee, *op. cit.*, p. 7.

24. Fryer, *op. cit.*, pp. 382 *et seq.*

25. For fuller account see *Ch'ing Shih Kao*, Hsüan Chü, Chih 2, *passim*.

26. Petitions from reformers in non-official circles such as K'ang Yu-wei and Liang Ch'i-ch'ao had due effect in moving official China along the path of reform. For the influence of these outstanding reformers especially, see Franke, O., *Ostasiatische Neubildungen*, pp. 23 *et seq.*

27. Faber, Dr. Ernst (Hua Chih An), *Tê Kuo Hsüeh Hsiao Lun Lüeh*, 1873, Reprinted by the Commercial Press in 1897 as the *T'ai Hsi Hsüeh Hsiao Lun Lüeh* (Western Schools and Principles of Education), Vide "A Classified Index to the Chinese Literature of the Protestant Churches in China," Shanghai, 1918, p. 167.
28. Martin, W. A. P., *Hsi Hsüeh K'ao Lüeh* ("A Résumé of Western Education"), Peking, 1883.
29. Candler, Warren A., *Young J. Allen*, pp. 174-75. As editor of the *Wan Kwoh Kung Pao*, or ("Review of the Times,") which he published monthly from 1868 to 1907, he was able to exert a very great influence. He also published some thirty volumes of translations as well as original works. For a list of these see pp. 170-72 of the biography.
30. Jackson, J., "Objects, Methods and Results of Higher Education in our Mission Schools," *Chinese Recorder*, XXIV (1893), 7 *et seq.* For a list of books written or translated into Chinese by missionaries in this period see *Records of the Missionary Conference*, Shanghai, 1890, pp. 715 *et seq.* and *A Classified Index to the Chinese Literature of the Protestant Churches in China*, Shanghai, 1918. Also consult Latourette, K. S., *A History of Christian Missions in China*, pp. 429 *et seq.*
31. Ferguson, John C., "Higher Education in China," *Chinese Recorder*, XXIII (1892), 154.
32. Parker, A. P., "The Government Colleges of Suchow," *Chinese Recorder*, XXIV (1893), 538.
33. *Draft History of the Ch'ing Dynasty*, Hsüan Chü, Chih 2, *passim.*
34. Parker, *op. cit.*, pp. 579-83.
35. *Ibid.*, p. 584.

CHAPTER II

1. Vide Tse Tsan Tai, *The Chinese Republic;* Sun Yat-sen, *Memoirs of a Chinese Revolutionary;* Maybon, Albert, *La Politique Chinoise.*
2. Ko, Kung-chên, *Chung Kuo Pao Hsüeh Shih* ("History of Chinese Journalism"), *passim;* Wang, Y. P., *Rise of the Native Press in China, passim.*
3. *Kwang Hsü Tung Hwa Hsü Lu* (Governmental documents, 1875-1908), chüan 132-142. *passim.*

4. The *Shu Yüan* or Provincial Colleges were located in the various provincial capitals. Those in attendance were advanced scholars usually having the *chü-jên* degree, roughly equivalent to our Master's degree. They studied there in preparation for the higher examinations. These colleges represented in the provinces the position assigned to the Kuo Tzŭ Chien (National College) in the capital. They were usually financed by provincial revenues, while students received nominal stipends. (See Mayers, W. F., *The Chinese Government*, Shanghai, 1886, pp. 75, 76).

5. Hail, W. J., *Tsêng Kuo-fan and the T'aip'ing Rebellion*, pp. 1-16; Mayers, W. F., *The Chinese Government*, pp. 51-61.

6. *Tung Hua Lu*, chüan 133, pp. 12, 13.

7. *Ibid.*, chüan 132, pp. 16, 17; Shu, Hsin-ch'êng, *op. cit.*, 1, 22, 23; *vide supra*, p. 12.

8. *Ibid.*, chüan 134, pp. 24, 25, 26.

9. Woodbridge, Samuel I., *China's Only Hope;* Tobar, Jérome, Le Père, *K'iuen-Hio P'ien*, Exhortations a l'étude par S. Exc. Tchang Tche-tong. Dr. John C. Ferguson who was associated with Chang's Yamen in these years confirms my statement that Chang was the editor and not the author of the essays.

10. *Tung Hua Lu*, chüan 132, pp. 6. 7.

11. The Four Books were: the *Ta Hsüeh* ("Great Learning"), the *Chung Yung* ("Doctrine of the Mean"), the *Lun Yü* ("Conversations of Confucius"), and *Mêng-tzu* ("Sayings of Mencius").

12. The Five Classics were: the *I Ching* or "Book of Changes," the *Shih Ching* or "Book of Poetry," the *Shu Ching*, or "Book of History," the *Li Chi* or "Canon of Rites" and the *Ch'un Ch'iu* or "The Spring and Autumn Annals."

13. *Tung Hua Lu*, chüan 134.

14. *Ibid.*, chüan 136, pp. 10-14.

15. *Ibid.*, chüan 138, pp. 1-4.

16. *Ibid.*, chüan 141, pp. 11, 12 and chüan 140, p. 17.

17. *Ibid.*, chüan 142, pp. 6-8.

18. Shu, Hsin-ch'êng, *op. cit.*, IV, 134 *et seq.*

19. Hu Shih, *The Chinese Renaissance*, Chinese Association for the Advancement of Education, Bulletin 6 (1923), Vol. II, *passim; vide* Wong Yun-wu, Ed., *Yen I Ming Chu Ts'ung K'an*, (Yen Fu's Translated Works), 8 vols., Commercial Press, 1931. Yen Fu's principal translations were as follows: J. S. Mill's, *On*

Liberty (*"Ch'ün Chi Ch'üan Chieh Lun"*), 1899 and *System of Logic* (*"Mu Lê Ming Hsüeh"*), 1902; H. Spencer's *Study of Sociology* (*"Ch'ün Hsüeh I Yen"*), 1902; Adam Smith's *Wealth of Nations* (*"Yüan Fu"*), 1902; C. D. S. Montesquieu's, *L'Esprit des lois* (*"Fa I"*), 1902; E. Jenks, *History of Politics* (*"Shê Hui Tung Ch'üan"*), 1903; Henry Huxley's *Evolutional Ethics and Other Essays* (*"T'ien Yen Lun"*), 1905; and U. S. Jevons, *Elements of Logic* (*"Ming Hsüeh Ch'ien Shuo"*), 1908.

20. Shu, Hsin-ch'êng, *op. cit.*, IV, 148-150; I, 23-35.
21. *Ibid.*, I, 37 *et seq.*
22. Nanyang University 1925-26, *Catalogue for the 30th Year*, pp. 3, 4.
23. Ferguson, John C., *Nanyang Graduation Address*, 1903.
24. *Shanghai Mercury*, July 14, 1903.
25. Shu, Hsin-ch'êng, *op. cit.*, I, 40 *et seq.*, and 64-66.
26. Morse, H. B. *The International Relations of the Chinese Empire*, III, 137 *et seq. Vide* Shu, Hsin-cheng, *op. cit.*, I, 73 *et seq.;* King, H. E., *The Educational System of China as Recently Reconstructed*, pp. 19-29; Tobar, *Décrets Impériaux*, 1898, Serie d' Orient, No. 4, Shanghai, 1900.
27. On the Boxer crisis especially see Cordier, H., "Les Origines de la Revolution en Chine," *T'oung Pao*, Series II, vol. I, number 5; and Steiger, G. N., *China and the Occident.*
28. Shu, Hsin-ch'êng, *op. cit.*, I, 78.
29. *Ibid.*, 78, *et seq.*
30. System of promoting candidates for degrees by classes. Originated under T'ang and copied by the Ming and Ch'ing dynasties.
31. The Six Arts were: Ceremonial Observances; Music; Archery; Charioteering; Writing; Mathematics.
32. The Nine Abilities were the ability: 1. To divine with the tortoise shell; 2. To conduct the hunt; 3. To engrave inscriptions on the (bronze) vessels; 4. To discharge one's mission as an ambassador; 5. To compose poetry in high mountain retreats; 6. To address troops; 7. To discourse on landscapes; 8. To pronounce eulogies over the dead; and 9. To conduct sacrificial services.
33. Members of a strong Central Asian tribe most powerful at that time.
34. See *Sui Shih*, Chüan 32, Ching Chi Chih, Ching Pu I.

35. *Vide Ch'in Ting Szu K'u Ch'üan Shu Tsung Mu,* Chüan 41, Ching Pu, Hsiao Hsüeh Lei, second section.
36. The *T'zŭ Yüan* states that this system of marking on the basis of accumulated grades resulting from frequent periodic examinations was employed under the Yüan dynasty (1280-1368) by the *Kuo Tzŭ Chien* or National College. However, according to the *Sung Shih* ("History of the Sung Dynasty") Chüan 157, Hsüan Chü Chih, this system was employed in the Sung period.
37. *Kwang Hsü Chêng Yao,* XXIII, 19 *et seq.*
38. *Ching Pao, loc. cit.,* approximately according to the date of the decrees.
39. *Ibid.*
40. *Ibid.*
41. *Ibid.*
42. *Vide supra,* pp. 25 *et seq.*
43. In the years following 1872, it will be recalled (p. 9), 120 young Chinese boys of the ages from twelve to fifteen were selected to go at governmental expense to the United States to study for a period of fifteen years. They were all hurriedly recalled in 1881 chiefly because the conservatives felt they were losing all their Chinese culture and becoming Americanized. Hence the admonition now, that they be well versed in Chinese literature. Within recent years the conviction has grown up that students of college age should not be sent abroad for study as long residence in a foreign land at such tender years unfits them for effective life in China upon their return.
44. King, H. E., *op. cit.,* p. 14; Yung Wing, *My Life in China and America,* pp. 170 *et seq.; Ching Pao, loc. cit.*
45. *Ching Pao, loc. cit.* and *Ch'ing Shih Kao,* Hsüan Chü, Chih 2, p. 5.
46. King, H. E., *op. cit.,* p. 33.
47. *Vide, Chinese Recorder,* XXV (1894), 295. These unused portions of indemnity money were paid the U. S. Government by the Chinese as retribution for a series of assaults, extending over several decades, upon Americans in China, or their property.
48. Duncan, Moir, "The Imperial University of Shansi," *East of Asia,* III (1904), 102.
49. Shu, Hsin-ch'êng, *op. cit.,* I, 66-72.
50. Duncan, Moir, *op. cit.,* 102 *et seq.*

51. Preston, T. J., "Progress and Reform in Hunan Province," *East of Asia,* IV (1905), 215, 217.

52. It is interesting to note in this connection that in April, 1898 when the examinations were being held in Peking, Liang Ch'i-ch'ao, the reformer, tried to collect signatures for a petition for the abolition of the *Pa-ku-wen-chang* or eight-legged essay. He was not very successful as the students then in Peking had no desire to throw away the fruits of their labor.

53. Shu, Hsin-ch'êng, *op. cit.,* IV, 117 *et seq.*

54. *Ibid.,* 121 *et seq.*

55. Westerners played a direct part in the abolition of the old examination system through provisions in the Boxer Protocol suspending for five years these examinations in a number of cities where outbreaks against foreigners had occurred. Forty-five cities were enumerated including Peking itself.

56. Shu, Hsin-ch'êng, *op. cit.,* IV, 124 *et seq.*

57. *Ibid.; Kwang Hsü Chêng Yao,* chüan 31.

58. Shu, Hsin-ch'êng, *op. cit.,* IV, 128.

59. Kuo, Ping-wen, *The Chinese System of Public Education,* pp. 78 *et seq.*

60. Kuno, Y. S., *Educational Institutions in the Orient,* part II, ("Chinese Educational Institutions"), pp. 9-13.

61. Kuo, Ping-wên, *op. cit.,* p. 80; *Ch'in Ting Ch'u Têng Hsiao Hsüeh T'ang Chang Chêng* ("Official regulations governing primary schools"), published by *Ch'ing Shih Kuan Shu Chü Yin,* p. 1 and p. 4, *et seq.*

62. Kuo, *op. cit.,* p. 81 and *Ch'in Ting Chung Hsüeh T'ang Chang Chêng* ("Official regulations governing middle schools"), p. 1 *et seq.*

63. *Vide supra.,* p. 4.

64. Harada, J., "Japanese Educational Influence in China," *Records of the Fifth Meeting of the Educational Association of China,* pp. 101-105.

65. Reid, Gilbert, "Educational Literature," *Records of the Fifth Meeting of the Educational Association of China,* p. 338.

66. Ko, Kung-chên, *Chung Kuo Pao Hsüeh Shih* ("History of Chinese Journalism"), pp. 121-141.

67. *Chiao Yü Shih Chieh* ("The Educational World"), May, June, July, 1901. Also see *Chiao Yü Ts'ung Shu Ch'u Chi* ("Miscel-

laneous collection of educational documents"), 10 vols., 1901.
68. Lo Chên-yü ("The Five Educational Requirements"), *Chiao Yü Shih Chieh*, Sept., 1901, pp. 1-3.
69. Tsuji, Takeo, "China's Educational Revolution", *Chiao Yü Shih Chieh*, June, 1901, pp. 1-3.
70. For a brief, but excellent account of Liang's works, his life and his thought consult D'Elia, Pascal M., "Un Mâitre de la jeune Chine: Liang K'i-Tch'ao," *T'oung Pao*, XVIII (1917), 247 *et seq.*
71. Yen, W. W., "Chinese Students in Japan," *East of Asia*, IV (1905), 194.
72. Consult *Yin Ping Shih Wên Chi Ch'üan Pien* ("The Collected writings of Liang Ch'i-ch'ao"), 20 vols., especially vols. VIII and IX. Also see the *Hsin Min Ts'ung Pao Hui* ("The New People's Journal"), *passim*.
73. Liang, Ch'i-ch'ao, "The Aims of the Modern Hunan School," Translated by Evan Morgan in *Wenli Styles and Chinese Ideals*, pp. 214-240.
74. Darroch, John, "The Present State of Literature in China," *Records of the Fifth Meeting of the Educational Association of China*, p. 194.
75. Lyon, Willard, "One Phase of the New Education in China," *East of Asia*, IV (1905), pp. 318 *et seq.* (Taken from the *Kuo Min Pi Tu.*)
76. *Ibid.*, p. 320.
77. *Ibid.*, p. 325.
78. The *Chêng Wu Ch'u* was established in 1901 for the purpose of examining reports and memorials dealing with reforms, coming from both the officials and the people. In 1905 the Bureau was reorganized as the *Nei Ko Hui I Chêng Wu Ch'u* when the number of its members was increased.
79. The *Hsüeh Wu Ch'u* was established in 1903 and expanded in 1905 into the Ministry of Education. The first members of this Committee were Chang Pai-hsi, Yung Ch'ing and Chang Chih-tung. Two of these men and Sun Chia-nai presented to the Throne the plan for the first modern system of education for China. *Vide Supra*, p. 50.
80. Located in Peking. Also called the "Imperial Academy of Learning." For a description of its internal organization see Brunnert

and Hagelstrom, *Present Day Political Organization of China,* pp. 136 *et seq.* and the *Ch'ing Shih Kao,* Hsüan Chü, Chih 1, p. 2.

81. Kuo, Ping-wên, *op. cit.,* pp. 87, 88; also see Brunnert, N. S. and Hagelstrom, V. V., *Present day Political Organization of China,* pp. 274, 395, 574, 828, 941.

82. Monroe, Paul, *Report on Education in China,* p. 9.

83. Kuo, *op. cit.,* pp. 88, 89.

84. *Vide supra,* p. 50.

85. Cf. Morse, H. B., *op. cit.,* III, 417.

86. Shu, Hsin-ch'êng, *op. cit.,* II, 96-102.

87. King, H. E., *op. cit.,* pp. 51-53. For a more detailed account of the educational system as adopted in 1903 and developed to 1910, see Brunnert and Hagelstrom, *op. cit.,* pp. 211-266.

88. King, *op. cit.,* p. 54.

89. *Ibid.,* p. 59.

90. Chinese National Association for the Advancement of Education, *Statistical Summaries of Chinese Education,* Vol. II (1923), Bulletin 16, pp. 1, 2.

91. Graybill, Henry B., *The Educational Reform in China,* pp. 63, 64.

92. *Ibid.,* pp. 64, 66.

Chapter III

1. Yin, Chiling, *Reconstruction of Modern Educational Organizations in China,* pp. 35, 40, *et seq.*

2. Shu, Hsin-ch'êng, *op. cit.,* IV, 195-198.

3. Kuo, P. W., *op. cit.,* p. 112.

4. *Chiao Yü Pu Wên Tu Hui Pien* ("Collected documents of the Ministry of Education"), I, 4.

5. *Ibid.,* p. 7.

6. Kuo, P. W., *op. cit.,* p. 114.

7. *Ibid.*

8. Shu, Hsin-ch'êng, *op. cit.,* IV, 26-32.

9. *Ibid.,* pp. 32-34.

10. *Chiao Yü Pu Wên Tu Hui Pien,* I, 23.

11. *Ibid.,* I, 81.

12. *Ibid.,* III, 54 *et seq.*

13. *Chiao Yü Kung Pao,* ("Official periodical of the Ministry of Education"), Vol. I, no. 5, pp. 2, 3.

14. *Chiao Yü Tsa Chih* ("Chinese Educational Review"), Vol. VII, no. 2, pp. 37-41.
15. *Chiao Yü Pen Wên Tu Hui Pien,* III, 119-20.
16. *Ibid.,* pp. 103, 104, 117.
17. Shu, Hsin-ch'êng, *op. cit.,* II, 113-120.
18. *Ibid.,* p. 120.
19. *Vide supra,* pp. 50, 51.
20. Kuno, Y. S., Educational Institutions in the Orient, Part II, *Chinese Educational Institutions,* pp. 9-13.
21. *Ibid.,* p. 16.
22. Shu, Hsin-ch'êng, *op. cit.,* pp. 116-117. "Society" and "nation" appear here to be practically synonymous terms.
23. *Chiao Yü Kung Pao,* February, 1919, Section on Current Affairs, pp. 1-8.
24. *Ibid.,* pp. 12-14.
25. *Ibid.,* pp. 3-5.
26. *Chiao Yü Pu Wên Tu Hui Pien,* V, 72-77.
27. *Ibid.,* p. 78.
28. *Ibid.,* p. 52.
29. *Chiao Yü Kung Pao,* Vol. VII, no. 7, July, 1920, Current Affairs Section, pp. 1 *et seq.*
30. *Ibid.*
31. *Ibid.,* Vol. VIII, June, 1921, Current Affairs Section, pp. 1-7; *Vide infra,* pp. 88, 90 92, and 95, for further mention of education among Mongolians and Tibetans.
32. *Ibid.*
33. *Ibid.*
34. Wang, Tsi, C., *The Youth Movement in China.*
35. *Chiao Yü Tsa Chih,* Vol. XVI, no. 8 (Aug., 1924), pp. 1-6.
36. *Hsin Chiao Yü* ("The New Education"), Vol. IX, no. 3 (Oct., 1924). Special number on the third annual conference of the Association for the Advancement of Education, pp. 675-708.
37. *Ibid.,* Vol. IX, No. 5 (Dec., 1924), Special number on the Educational Exhibition.
38. *Chiao Yü Tsa Chih,* Vol. XVII, no. 12 (Dec., 1925), Section on Educational Affairs, pp. 4 *et seq.*
39. *Hsin Chiao Yü,* Vol. XI, no. 2 (Sept., 1925), pp. 147, 148.
40. *Ibid.,* pp. 209 *et seq.*
41. *Ibid.,* pp. 243, 244.

42. *Ibid.*, pp. 235-237.
43. *Ibid.*, pp. 250 *et seq.*
44. The University Council (Compiler), *Ch'üan Kuo Chiao Yü Hui I Pao Kao,* (National Educational Conference Report), pp. 2, 3.
45. *Ibid.*, pp. 3, 4.
46. *Ibid.*, pp. 459, *et seq.* especially pp. 468, 475, 18.
47. *Ibid.*, p. 586. For the change in textbooks see Appendix I, Numbers xiii, xxvii-xxxii, xl and xli.
48. *Ibid.*, pp. 182, 185.
49. *Ibid.*, p. 186.
50. *Ibid.*, pp. 340 *et seq.;* especially p. 345.
51. *Ibid.*, pp. 170 *et seq.*
52. *Ibid.*, p. 291.
53. *Ibid.*, pp. 41 and 29.

CHAPTER IV

1. Darroch, John, "Chinese Textbooks," *Journal of the North China Branch Royal Asiatic Society,* XXXVII (1906), 211.
2. *Chiao Yü Pu Pien Tsuan Ku Yüeh K'an,* Vol. II, ch. 1, p. 32.
3. *Chaio Yü Pu Wên Tu Hui Pien,* Vol. II (Jan., 1914), Decrees number 7 and 8.
4. *Vide* App., Digest of textbooks, nos. XV, XVI, XVII, XVIII, XIX, XX, XXXV, XXXVI, XLIV, XLV.
5. *Chiao Yü Pu Wên Tu Hui Pien,* I, 34 *et seq.*
6. *Ibid.*, p. 34.
7. *Vide supra,* Note 4.
8. *Chiao Yü Pu Wên Tu Hui Pien, op. cit.*, pp. 35, 36.
9. *Ibid.*, p. 36.
10. *Ibid.*, p. 38.
11. *Ibid.*, pp. 39, 40.
12. *Chiao Yü Pu Ling Hui Pien,* (1913, Order no. 16.) Collected decrees and orders of the Ministry of Education.
13. *Chiao Yü Kung Pao, 1913,* no. 7, App., pp. 11, 12.
14. *Ibid.*, pp. 36, 49.
15. *Chiao Yü Pu Ling Hui Pien,* 1913, pp. 52-54.
16. *Chiao Yü Kung Pao,* Vol. 1, no. 1, Section on public documents, p. 2.
17. *Ibid.*, pp. 2 *et seq.*
18. *Chiao Yü Pu Wên Tu Hui Pien,* III, 168.

19. *Vide* App., Digest of textbooks no. XXI.
20. The older term "Kuo Min" means literally the people of the nation. When the legalistic conception of citizenship arose after 1918, the term "Kung Min" meaning the public as opposed to the private, or family, functions of the people came into common use. A few educators at this time may have grasped the western conception of citizenship, but only a few. For example see article by Ts'ai Yüan-p'ei in which he employs the term "Kung Min." But his use of the term was exceptional. (See Shu, Hsin-ch'êng, *op. cit.*, IV, 26 ff.)
21. *Chiao Yü Kung Pao*, Vol. VII, no. 7, July, 1920, Section on current affairs, pp. 1 *et seq.*
22. *Loc. cit.*
23. The term for "character" here is *p'in hsing*. See *The Chinese Cyclopedia of Education*, I, 697-700 for an explanation and discussion of this term based on a summary of A. F. Shand's, *The Foundations of Character*.
24. *Hsin Chiao Yü*, Vol. XI, no. 2 (Sept., 1925), pp. 267-270.
25. *Loc. cit.*
26. *Ibid.*, pp. 275-277.
27. *Ibid.*, Vol. VII, nos. 2 & 3 (Oct., 1923), pp. 118-119.
28. *Ibid.*, p. 127.
29. Luh, C. W., "China's New System of Education," In Chinese National Association for the Advancement of Education, Vol. II (1923), Bulletin 8, p. 1.
30. Kuno, Y. S., *op. cit.*, p. 29. Also see Liao, S. C., "Middle School Education in China," In Chinese National Association for the Advancement of Education, *op. cit.*, Bulletin 12, p. 13.
31. Cheng, Tsung-hai, "Elementary Education in China," In Chinese National Association for the Advancement of Education, *op. cit.*, Bulletin 14, p. 15 and the App. Also see the *Hsin Chiao Yü*, Vol. VII, nos. 2 & 3 (Oct., 1923), pp. 121 *et seq.*
32. King, Chu, "The Reorganization of the Middle School Curriculum," In National Association for the Advancement of Education, *op. cit.*, Bulletin 13, p. 2.
33. *Ibid.*, p. 3.
34. *Ibid.*, pp. 3, 4.
35. *Ibid.*, p. 4.
36. *Ibid.*, p. 5.

37. Chuang, Chai H., "Movement for Educating Illiterates in China," In Chinese National Association for the Advancement of Education, *op. cit.*, Bulletin 2, pp. 21, 22.
38. *Vide supra*, pp. 89 *et seq.*
39. Li, Kuan-ch'ing, In the *Chung Hwa Educational Review*, Vol. XV (Aug., 1925), no. 2.
40. *China Weekly Review*, Sept. 13, 1930, p. 64.

CHAPTER V

1. Hayes, Carlton, J. H., *Essays on Nationalism*, pp. 1-29, especially p. 26, and *The Historical Evolution of Modern Nationalism, passim.*
2. It is not here implied that China did not have a School of Law (*Fa Chia*). This school developed under the stress of the struggle of the Warring Kingdoms during the period from 500-200 B.C. Though instrumental in the establishment of the Han dynasty and the overthrow of feudalism, this task once accomplished the school was doomed to fall. Its great rival Confucianism with its emphasis on rule by *"li,"* or custom rooted in natural moral law, superseded the concept of a rule by *"fa,"* or artificially created norms of conduct. "The crude attempts of the School of Law to regulate life by man-made law (it was the Legalists who urged Ch'in Shih Huang Ti to burn all books which dealt with past manners, customs and rights in 213 B.C.) has scared the Chinese mind away from attempts in that direction, even from codification of the existing customary law, from any other point of view than that of penal." In China ". . . law became again firmly embedded in ethics. . . ." Only such law as was in harmony with established custom was observed by the Chinese. Innovations were immoral. In such an atmosphere the abstract concept of a sovereign state equal among others could not develop; indeed was antithetical to the prevailing conception, through the centuries, of the Empire as being universally supreme and without equal. *Vide* Dr. J. J. L. Duyvendak, *The Book of Lord Shang*, London, 1928, pp. 124-130.
3. Jackson, J., "Objects, Methods and Results of Higher Education in our Mission Schools," *Chinese Recorder*, XXIII (1892), 556-563.

The Rev. Jackson here sets forth the type of education which he feels the missionaries should provide:

1. They should aim to give a good education, even though their primary aim is to make Christians of the students.
2. *They should not foreignize the students.*
3. They should endeavor to develop among the students the spirit of patriotism and in that connection he writes, "Patriotism is not a very prevalent virtue in China, and enlightened patriotism hardly exists" (p. 559). Therefore mission schools should impart their education chiefly through the medium of the Chinese language.

4. Pelliot, Paul, *Le Mouvement réformiste en Chine*, pp. 6 *et seq;* K'ang Yu-wei, *"Chin Ch'êng Jih Pên Ming Chih Pien Chêng K'ao Hsü," K'ang Nan Hai Chi*, 1912, chüan 8, pp. 29 *et seq.*
5. Ch'ên Ch'i-t'ien *Chung Kuo Hsin Chiao Yü Szü Ch'ao Hsiao Shih, Chung Hua Chiao Yü Chieh* ("Résumé of the thought tides of the new education in China"), Vol. XIII, no. 2 (Aug., 1923), p. 8.
6. Liang Ch'i-ch'ao, *Yin Ping Shih Wên Chi Ch'üan Pien* ("Collected Works"), *passim.*
7. Trans. from the *Yin Ping Shih Ts'ung Chu*, Book I, pp. 190 *et seq.*, by J. J. L. Duyvendak in *Over Chineesche Oorlogsgoden*, pp. 35, 36.
8. Darroch, John, "The Present State of Literature in China," Records of the Fifth Meeting of the Educational Association of China, pp. 194 *et seq.*
9. Tobar, Le Père Jérome, *K'iuen-Hio P'ien*, pp. 4, 5.
10. *"Kuo Chia Chu I Yü Chiao Yü," Hsin Chiao Yü*, Feb., 1924, pp. 27 *et seq.*
11. Liang Ch'i-ch'ao, *"Lun Chiao Yü Tang Ting Tsung Chih," Yin Ping Shih Wên Chi Ch'üan Pien*, chüan 9, p. 1 *et seq.*
12. *Yü Chia-chü, "Chiao Yü Shang Ti Kuo Chia Chu I Yü Ch'i T'a San Chung Chu I Chih Pi Chiao."*
13. *"Hu An Yü Chiao Yü," Chung Kuo Chiao Yü Chieh*, Aug., 1925.
14. Chiang, Monlin, *A Study in the Chinese Principles of Education*, pp. 182, 183, 186, 187.
15. Ts'ai Yüan-P'ei, *"Chiao Yü Chih Tui Tai Ti Fa Chan"* ("Developing Educational Objectives"), *Hsin Chiao Yü*, February, 1919, pp. 9, 10.

16. *Vide supra,* p. 76 *et seq.*
17. Yen, Y. C. James, "How to Educate China's Illiterate Millions for Democracy in a Decade," Chinese Association for the Advancement of Education, *op. cit.,* Bulletin 15, p. 21.
18. Yen, Y. C. James, *The Mass Education Movement in China,* pp. 24, 25.
19. *Vide supra,* p. 93.
20. The history of the origin and adoption of the *San Min Chu I* is of interest. Pascal M. D'Elia S. J. in his work *Le Triple Démisme de Suen Wen* (Shanghai: Zi-ka-we, 1930), pp. 16-17, states that it was formed in Sun Yat-sen's mind during his travels in the United States and Europe, in 1896-98, in the course of which he read Lincoln's Gettysburg Oration. The idea of a government of the people, by the people and for the people impressed him. However, in the proclamation of the *Hsing Chung Hui* issued in 1894, we find the rudiments of the three principles expressed. The term *Min Shêng* (People's Livelihood) being actually employed. (*Vide, Chung Shan Ts'ung Shu,* Shanghai, *San Min Shu Tien,* Vol. IV, section *Li Nien Chêng Chih Hsüan Yen,* pp. 1, *et seq.*) In the proclamation of the *T'ung Meng Hui,* organized in 1905, we find the principles clearly set forth together with the three periods or stages of development. (Vide *Chung Shan Ts'ung Shu, op. cit.,* p. 4 *et seq.;* D'Elia, *op. cit.* p. 20.) These three principles, together with the five-power Constitution were discoursed on at some length by Sun at Tokyo in January 1907 on the occasion of the anniversary of the *Min Pao* or "The People's Newspaper." (*Vide* Bulletin de l'Ecôle Française de l'Extrême Orient, VII, 442 *et seq.;* Also III, 759 and reviews by Prof. T. F. Tsiang of Tsing Hua University in the *Chinese Social and Political Science Review* for Apr., 1931, of Tsou Lu's *A Preliminary History of the Kuomintang* and Hu Han-min (Ed.) *Collected Writings of Dr. Sun Yat-sen;* pp. 102 *et seq.* especially p. 107 for further confirmation of above statements).
21. Sun Yat-sen, *San Min Chu I,* Shanghai, 1924. The edition consulted was the 18th published in the collection *Chung Shan Ts'ung Shu, Shanghai,* 1928, 4 vols.; Price, Frank W., *The Three Principles of the People.* (This translation is relied upon here, though retranslations were made at a few points where the

author disagreed). Also see D'Elia, Pascal M., S. J., *Le Triple Démisme de Suen Wen*, Shanghai, 1930, *passim*.

22. Price, Frank W., *op. cit.*, p. ix.
23. *Ibid.*, pp. 3, 4.
24. *Ibid.*, pp. 11, 12.
25. *Ibid.*, pp. 68, 69, 75, 76.
26. *Ibid.*, pp. 98, 99.
27. *Ibid.*, p. 115.
28. *Ibid.*, p. 133.
29. *Ibid.*, pp. 178, 179.
30. *Ibid.*, p. 181.
31. *Ibid.*, p. 364.
32. *Chiao Yü Pu Wên Tu Hui Pien*, I, 59.
33. *Ibid.*, pp. 69, 144.
34. *Chiao Yü Kung Pao*, July 20, 1921, Section on official documents, p. 1; Section on official letters, p. 14; Section on current affairs, pp. 10, 11.
35. *Chiao Yü Pu Wên Tu Hui Pien*, III (Dec., 1918), p. 134.
36. Chuang, Chai H., *op. cit.*, p. 8.
37. Tyau, M. T. Z., *Two Years of Nationalist China*, Shanghai, 1930, Preface.
38. *Kwang Hsü Chêng Yao*, XXIII, 27 *et seq.*
39. *Vide Supra*, p. 57.
40. Ko, Kung-chên, *op. cit.*, pp. 115 *et seq.*
41. Liu, Fu, *Les Mouvements de la langue nationale en Chine*, p. 3.
42. Hu Shih, "The Chinese Renaissance," Chinese Association for the Advancement of Education, *op. cit.*, Bulletin 6, pp. 25-28.
43. Cp. Liu, Fu, *op. cit.*, pp. 6-7.
44. Li, Chin-hsi, "Historical Survey of the National Language Movement and its Policy," *Chiao Yü Kung Pao*, Jan., 1919, pp. 1-29, Lecture section; Latourette, K. S., *History of Christian Missions in China*, pp. 264-266, 429-435.
45. Liu, Fu, *op. cit.*, p. 14. Prof. J. J. L. Duyvendak has informed the writer that K'ang Yu-wei advocated the teaching of the *Kuo Yü* to unify the country. From 1900 on, Chinese schools in Java, established under K'ang Yu-wei's influence, taught Mandarin, although this was a foreign language to the children of the Chinese there who had almost without exception come from the southern provinces.
46. Li, Chin-hsi, *op. cit.*, pp. 11, 12.

47. Liu, Fu, *op. cit.*, pp. 13-20.
48. Li, Chin-hsi, *op. cit.*, pp. 12, 13.
49. Hu Shih, *op. cit.*, pp. 30 *et seq.*; and Liu, Fu, *op. cit.*, pp. 44 *et seq.*; Duyvendak, J. J. L., "A Literary Renaissance in China," *Acta Orientalia*, 1923; Demieville, P; "Hou Che Wen Ts'ouen," *Bulletin de l'Ecôle Française de l'Extrême Orient*, XXIII (1923), 492.
50. Li, Chin-hsi, *op. cit.*, p. 13.
51. *Chiao Yü Kung Pao*, Vol. VI, no. 9 (Sept., 1919), section on Miscellaneous items, p. 26.
52. Hu Shih, *op. cit.*, p. 32.
53. De Vargas, P. H., "Some Elements in the Chinese Renaissance," *New China Review*, IV (1922), 243.
54. Wieger, Père Leon, *Chine Moderne*, 7 vols. See especially, Vol. V, *Nationalisme, Xenophobie, Anti-christianisme*, 1924; and Vol. VI, *Le Feu aux poudres*, 1925; and Vol. VII, *Boum!* 1926-27. These volumes are made up entirely of translations or summaries of leading articles in the outstanding periodicals of China during the years 1921-27. They make excellent source material.
55. Hu Shih, *op. cit.*, p. 29.
56. Doré, R. P. Henri, "Le Confucisme sous la Republique, 1911-22," *The New China Review*, IV (1922), 298-319, especially p. 299.
57. *Vide supra*, p. 46.
58. Tsu, Y. Y., "Present Tendencies in Chinese Buddhism," pp. 76-79. (In T. T. Lew *et al.*, *China Today through Chinese Eyes*.)
59. *Ibid.*, pp. 82-92, especially p. 92.
60. *Vide supra*, p. 64 *et seq. Vide* Steiger, G. Nye, "China's attempt to Absorb Christianity." *T'oung Pao*, XXIV (1925-26), 215 *et seq.*
61. Doré, *op. cit.*, p. 299.
62. *Loc. cit.*
63. *Vide supra*, p. 75 *et seq.*
64. Doré, *op. cit.*, p. 302. Mention should be made here of the activities of Ch'ên Huan-chang who after 1911 carried on through the "Confucian Society" active propaganda for Confucianism and performed sacrifices at the Confucian temple in Peking. One of his ideas was to make Confucius the founder of a religion on a par with Christianity.

65. *Ibid.,* p. 305.
66. Kuan Yü lived about the year 200 A.D. during the restless period that followed the fall of the Han dynasty. For centuries he has been known as the greatest military hero of Chinese history. During the 12th century he was given by the Emperor the posthumous title of "Prince." In 1594 he was put under the title of "Emperor" in the State worship as official "war-god." Everywhere temples were erected to him, even in Korea where he was highly revered. The Manchu dynasty lavished honors on this god. In 1856 it was decided that his worship should be made equal to that of Confucius as he was believed to have been instrumental the year before in leading the Imperial troops to a great victory over the T'ai-p'ing rebels. He was officially sacrificed to in the name of the Emperor on his birthday the 13th day of the fifth month and on a "lucky" day in the spring and in the fall. With the establishment of the Republic this official worship ceased as did all other forms of State worship practised under the Empire save for the brief revival under Yüan here surveyed.

Yüeh Fei is also an historical figure. He lived from 1103-1141 under the Sung dynasty and distinguished himself in the struggle against the invading Tartars. His life's motto, which he allowed to be tatooed on his back, was: "to serve my land with unflinching loyalty." Sometime after his death he was given a posthumous honorary title. He was not as popular as Kuan Yü, yet in a number of places there are temples in his honor.

These two heroic figures were worshipped together on specified days in the spring and in the autumn. In their temple at Peking, Yüan Shih-k'ai arranged on either side of them the twenty-four famous officers whom he vainly tried to canonize. (*Vide* Duyvendak, J. J. L., *Over Chineesche Oorlogsgoden,* pp. 18-20; Johnston, R. F. "Chinese Cult of Military Heroes," *New China Review,* Feb., 1921, pp. 4 *et seq.,* and April, 1921, pp. 79 *et seq.*

67. Doré, *op. cit.,* p. 309; Duyvendak, J. J. L., *op. cit.,* pp. 17, 18.
68. Doré, *op. cit.,* p. 313.
69. *Ibid.,* pp. 314-315.
70. The clause in the Manchu Code which prohibited Christianity from the time of Yung Chêng (1723-36) until 1870, appeared

in the fourth division Ritual Laws *(Li Lü)*, the book on Sacrifices *(Chi Szŭ)* and the Section called "Prohibiting Magicians and (other) Perverse Enterprizes" *(Chin Chih Shih Wu Hsieh Shu)* and confined to a supplmentary article. Though following the first treaties with the West, 1842-44, the Chinese Government engaged no longer to prohibit Christianity, it was not until by a decree of the Emperor T'ung Chih, 1870, that all restrictions against it were removed from the Code. (See *Ta Ch'ing Lü Li Hui Chi Pien Lan, chüan* 16, p. 6b, published by the Hupeh Hsien Chü, in 40 chüan and two supplements, 1870; Boulais, P. Guy, *Manuel du Code Chinois,* Shanghai, 1924, pp. 363 *et seq.*, and Staunton, Sir George T., *Ta Tsing Leu Lee,* London, 1810, pp. 175, 176, 532-537.)

71. *Vide supra,* pp. 44, 45, 54.
72. Latourette, K. S., *op. cit.,* p. 644.
73. *Chiao Yü Pu Ling Hui Pien,* Second year, pp. 29-31.
74. Latourette, *op. cit.,* p. 644.
75. Miao, Chester S., and Price, Frank W., "Religion and Character in Christian Middle Schools," *Educational Review,* Oct., 1929, p. 361.
76. Latourette, *op. cit.,* p. 695.
77. Shu, Hsin-ch'êng, *Shou Hui Chiao Yü Ch'üan Yün Tung* ("Restore the Educational Prerogatives Movement"), *passim.*
78. Stauffer, M. T. (Ed.) *The Christian Occupation of China,* p. 404.
79. *Ibid.;* also see Shu, Hsin-ch'êng, *op. cit.,* p. 42. Only about 5 per cent of the student population were attending Christian schools at this time.
80. Latourette, *op. cit.,* p. 697.
81. *Loc. cit.*
82. Lo, R. Y., *China's Revolution from the Inside,* pp. 100, 101.
83. Latourette, *op. cit.,* p. 697-698; Shu, Hsin-ch'êng, *op. cit., passim;* Tang, Leang-li, *China in Revolt,* pp. 57-78.
84. *China Christian Educational Quarterly,* Vol. I, no. 1, pp. 53-54.
85. *Ibid.,* p. 44.
86. Latourette, *op. cit.,* p. 698. See footnote here for references to the registration rules of 1912, 1921, etc.
87. Miao, C. S., and Price, F. W., *op. cit.,* p. 368.
88. *Ibid.,* p. 374.

89. In the *Provisional Constitution for the Period of Tutelage,*
    passed on May 12, 1931, by the National Convention of People's
    Representatives and promulgated by the National Government
    on June 1st, 1931, Ch. V, "Education," we find among others the
    two following articles:
    "Article 47. The Three Principles of the People shall be the
    basic principles of education in the Republic of China.
    Article 49. All public and private educational institutions in
    the country shall be subject to the supervision of the State and
    shall be responsible for the carrying out of the educational poli-
    cies adopted by the State." Quoted from the *Chinese Social and
    Political Science Review,* Vol. XV, no. 2 (July, 1931), p. 329.

INDEX

240 INDEX

Geography textbooks, 190-93; History textbooks, 165-68; Mass Education Movement textbooks, 159-65; National Readers, 180-90; Size of editions, 159

Tibetans, education, 76, 77, 86, 88, 91, 95

Translation, of Japanese works, 52, 53; of Western works, 5, 8, 9, 12, 25, 27, 30

Ts'ai Yüan-p'ei, 72, 80, 92, 128, 136, 141, 145

Tsên Ch'un-hsüan, 44, 47

Tsêng Kuo-fan, 5-8

Tsinan incident, 152

Tso Tsung-t'ang, 3, 5, 7, 8

Tsungli Yamen, 3, 25, 29, 30

T'ung Wên Kuan, 3, 4, 7, 12, 14, 21, 25, 29

United States, influence on Chinese school system, 74, 80, 85

Wang Kuo-wei, 53

Wang Wên-shao, 31

Wên Chang, 16; criticized, 17, 32, 47, 222

Wên Li, see Language

Wong Yün-wu, 98, 117

World Community, The, xiv, 102, 119; discussed in textbooks, 175; 176, 177, 178, 184, 188, 190

World's Student Christian Federation, meeting in Peking, 148

Wu Ching, 26

Wylie, Alexander, 5, 6, 9

Yen Fu, 30, 218, 219

Yen Hsi-shan, 114

Yen, James Y. C., 75, 129, 160

Yen, W. W., 56

Young China Association, The, 148

Yüan Shih-k'ai, 46, 47, 72, 77, 145, 146; biography of in textbook, 160

Yüeh Fei, 146, 232

Yung Ch'ing, 47, 60

Yung Wing, 8, 9